STILL STANDING

Inspirational Stories of Hope After Divorce

Inspired Grace Media Productions Llc.
Lexington, Kentucky

STILL STANDING:
Inspirational Stories of Hope After Divorce

Contributing Authors: Tammy Bolton, Shawna Dillon, Gina Erwin, Gwendolyn DiFerdinando, Teresa Robinson, Shelia Horton, and Charis Rooks.

Photographs Courtesy of: Tammy Bolton, Shawna Dillon, Gina Erwin, Gwendolyn DiFerdinando, Teresa Robinson, Shelia Horton, and Charis Rooks.
Contributing Editors: Alecia Wayman AW Inspired Edits, Gina Erwin, and Charis Rooks
Cover Design: Rebecca Garcia, Dark Wish Designs
Interior Layout/Graphic Design: Rebecca Garcia, Dark Wish Designs
Publishing Advocate: Gina Erwin, Inspired Grace Media Productions

PAPERBACK ISBN: 978-0-578-72412-6

The Cataloging-in-Publication Data is on file with the Library of Congress
Printed in the United States of America

First Edition
Special Sales
Most Inspired Grace Media books are available at special quantity discounts when purchased in bulk by corporations, organizations, and special-interest groups.
For information, please email info@igmproductions.com

Dedication

God, without you, I would not exist. Thank you for loving me and giving me a passion that guides me while on the journey of seeking my purpose daily.

Love,

Your Daughter Charis

CONTENTS

Charis Rooks

charis.rooks@igmproductions.com
charis.rooks@draw4women.com

As a two-time divorcee herself, Charis Rooks knows what it takes to rebuild a life after ending a marriage. Charis is an International Women's Leadership Coach, a Divorce Recovery Coach, as well as a Mental Health Coach. Charis has devoted her life to helping other women avoid the struggles that she went through following her divorces. She provides women with a platform, a voice, and a sympathetic ear so that they can recover and live the lives God created for them.

Charis has a bachelor's degree in Business and Technical Management, an MBA in Leadership, and is currently pursuant of a Doctor of Education in Christian Leadership and Ministry. Her doctoral research focuses on establishing an outreach prayer ministry for divorced women while equipping leaders to lead a prayer ministry. Charis is passionate about speaking the truth and working to spread the Word of God and its healing power. In addition to founding Divorce Recovery Advocates for Women, she is also the Editor in Chief/CEO of Inspired Grace Media Productions and the founder of Inspired Grace Ministries. She has served as a leader, coach, and Pastor in the Celebrate Recovery Ministry. Charis currently serves as the Discipleship and Prayer Pastor at Inspired Grace Ministries.

When she is not working to empower her fellow women, Charis loves spending time with her husband, daughters, and grandson. She and her family currently live in Kentucky.

Favorite Scripture:

Proverbs 3:5-6

"Trust in the LORD with all your heart and lean not on your own understanding; in all your ways submit to him, and he will make your paths straight."

Open Letter

As a woman who has been through divorce twice, I struggled tremendously during that season of my life. I hit rock bottom and even attempted to take my own life; little did I know, God had other plans for me. After giving my life to Christ as a last resort and seeking the help of God for my healing, I learned something. I was able to see how genuinely loved, worthy, and valuable I am to God.

After giving my life to Christ, I believe my passion for helping others with divorce recovery truly began. I understand from personal experience how our most unbearable and unimaginable pain can lead us to our exceptional testimony and love in life. Through Christ, anything is possible, be it recovery from divorce, or discovering your true calling and how God created us all with a desire to help others.

God has blessed me over the years with the opportunity to become a certified life coach, author, pastor, and even allowed me to help women in divorce recovery. These were the resources I wish I had been able to access when I was going through my divorces. It has been my goal to help other women become what they have always dreamed of and tap into their healing and power through their testimony.

I have had a passion for working with divorced women for many years now, and I hope that this book will help you on your journey. You could say that I have attended many divorce recovery programs, both in the role of participant, facilitator, and leader. Over time God has blessed me by allowing me the opportunity to hear the testimony of every woman that God has brought across my path. There came a time where I would ask each woman to share their story with other women that I had met to help them. I received so many responses from both sides about how much it helped them with their journey of personal healing. So, I prayed and asked God how I can take this to the next level as a writer? God answered and placed it on my heart to help teach and coach women on how they can write their testimonies and publish them. I wanted to take the testimonies that these women have and capture them in writing to bless not just the readers but also the authors on their spiritual journey of healing.

The power of testimony is far greater than even I could have imagined when I started this journey. Sharing your story can let others know that there is hope, there is a light after the darkest days of your life, and you can come out stronger and better for all the turmoil that you have suffered. Personal testimony is by large one of the best ways to relate to others and to truly honor God's work in your life while doing so.

This book is a result of answered prayer. A collection of testimonies from women that endured some of the most tragic times in their lives, yet they are still standing. They are the perfect representation of hope for those that might feel as if all hope is lost. These stories are written to inspire, empower, and motivate women who are going through separation or divorce to not give up on themselves and to keep going. With the right words of inspiration, you can overcome anything. You can be stronger, you can be more grounded, and blessed.

Divorce is not the end, and this book proves it. Though you might be struggling, you may be floundering to the point that you feel like you are drowning, there is hope, there is so much more out there for you, you just have to be willing to grab it. I know you have it in you to rise from the ruins and allow God to show you that you and your purpose is more beautiful than you ever imagined.

I pray this book finds you well

Blessings,

Charis Rooks

Charis Rooks
Founder-Divorce Recovery Advocates for Women
Editor in Chief/CEO-Inspired Grace Media Productions
Discipleship/Prayer Pastor-Inspired Grace Ministries

Words of Encouragement and Prayer Moving Forward

As a committed student of learning and God's Word, I have found His word to be encouraging, inspiring, and life-changing on my journey of brokenness. Though it may seem as if accepting God is hard, or challenging, His love can shine a light that you can only imagine. Developing my relationship with God has helped me through so many struggles in life and has helped to heal my heartbreak more times than I can count.

My prayer is that this book finds you and that it changes you. I pray that these testimonies help bless you and bring you closer to embracing and deepening your relationship with God and fulfilling your purpose in His will. No matter what your life circumstances may be, God is there for you, and He has a purpose for you, He has created a path for you, it is your responsibility to discover it.

This book was created to help show readers that there is hope, no matter how dark it may seem, no matter how far from the path you have strayed, there is life on the other side of divorce and the pain and struggle that it brings. God will guide you; you must open your heart and be willing to embrace Him fully. God loves you and that love is all that matters.

Blessings from Your Sister in Christ
Charis R.

Tammy Bolton

tammybolton.triimpact@gmail.com

Tammy is an anointed, inspirational, evocative teacher, and public speaker. Forged in the fire, she makes no apologies for her past or the scars she carries. Instead, she uses them to share her story of redemption and hope through authenticity and transparency.

Passionate to see women establish healthy, lasting relationships, she has ministered to women across the Midwest, founding encouragement ministries such as Mon Ami in Indiana, The Tribe in Ohio, and currently leads The Tribe in Kentucky. Shame and devastation from multiple failed marriages tried to discount and destroy her, but through God, she discovered He, alone, defines her. Walking in that truth, she is known as a "Warrior Queen" and a "Treasure Hunter" with a heart to see the broken, walking wounded, and shame-ridden set free. Her story is one of victory, the discovery of true worth, and a glorious testimony of how God gives beauty for ashes.

Favorite Scriptures

Isaiah 61:1-3 KJV

The Spirit of the Lord God is upon me; because the Lord hath anointed me to preach good tidings unto the meek; he hath sent me to bind up the brokenhearted, to proclaim liberty to the captives, and the opening of the prison to them that are bound; To proclaim the acceptable year of the Lord, and the day of vengeance of our God; to comfort all that mourn; To appoint unto them that mourn in Zion, to give unto them beauty for ashes, the oil of joy for mourning, the garment of praise for the spirit of heaviness; that they might be called trees of righteousness, the planting of the Lord, that he might be glorified.

Song of Solomon 6:3 (KJV)

I am my beloved's, and my beloved is mine

Inspired Grace Media

Dedication

Angela and Tressie, thank you for always believing in me and for refusing to allow me to be reduced to a victim of my past. To all the women who have been shrouded in shame, lost their voice, identity, dignity, and dreams. You are more than others' opinions of you and greater than the sum of your past mistakes. May God give you beauty for ashes.

Beauty for Ashes

By: Tammy Bolton

My story is a colorful story filled with misconceptions, fear, shame, guilt, promiscuity, abuse, and divorce. Let me assure you; I do not seek sympathy from anyone as you read these words. Although I would not wish what I have gone through over the past four decades on my worst enemy, I most definitely would wish the valuable lessons I have learned and the relationship I have now developed with God on every person in the world. My story is a story of Beauty for Ashes. If you are not familiar with that phrase, it is a scripture in the Bible, Isaiah 61:3, to be exact. The phrase *Beauty for Ashes* adequately sums of what you will discover in this chapter.

Up until about a year ago, I was ashamed to tell my story, but God has helped me work through the shame. I cannot begin to tell you the freedom I now feel. I will be candid with you, even when it is ugly. Please understand, I in no way want to give glory to the problems I have endured. Instead, I share the ugly things in hopes that you will find hope in the midst of whatever seemingly hopeless situation you are in as a result of your broken marriage. I pray you will come to understand the incredible love God has for you. Plagued with a gross misconception of who God is and how He feels about me, I doubted His love for me for most of my life. I also struggled with the root of rejection and performance-acceptance thinking. All these things caused me to make really poor choices that were rooted in fear, shame, and guilt, which are the ingredients for a painfully disappointing life, to say the least.

The Making of Embers #1 and #2

Let me tell you a little about myself. I grew up in a fundamental Christian home as the eldest of two daughters born of young parents, aged 19 and 17. Both of my parents came from low income, blue-collar and dysfunctional families where love was conditional and scarce. My parents did the best they knew how and gave me a much better childhood than either of them had experienced. I learned a plethora of knowledge from them, among which, the value of a dollar, work ethics, love for God, appreciation of nature, and the honor of one's word, just to name a few. They loved me to the best of their ability, yet I still ended up feeling like I was just one mistake away from losing their love and approval.

I do not plan to bore you with insignificant details of my childhood. I will share glimpses of time, that I have come to understand, where lies of the enemy, like small embers, were strategically planted by the enemy (Satan) in an attempt to destroy my confidence, distort my identity, and leave me in a pile of the charred remains of my life.

My first traumatic event happened when I was four. Satan thrives on wounding children while they are innocent, unassuming, and ill-equipped to fight. My family and I went to visit my aunt's house quite often, but this particular day was life-changing for me. I was in the back bedroom with two boys. One was the son of my aunt's brother-in-law; the other was the son of a neighbor. One was a year older than me, the other a year younger. I do not recall what prompted us to play "Doctor," but we did, and I was the patient. I was lying between the space between the wall and the bed, and they started giving me a full-body exam, both touching me. In walks, my mom and by the look on her face, I suddenly realized what we were doing was horribly wrong, although it was innocent. Mom grabbed me by the arm and started beating me, telling me how dirty and nasty **I** was. Although all three of us were equal participants in this incident, the boys never were scolded when their parents found out. **I** was the nasty one; this was **my** fault! That day a lie was planted in my brain, my soul, and my very core. That lie was **Ember #1; I am dirty and nasty**.

MY TRUTH: God says I am beautiful and clean.

You are altogether beautiful, my darling; beautiful in every way. - Song of Solomon 4:7 NLT

Purify me from my sins, and I will be clean; wash me, and I will be whiter than snow. - Psalms 51:7 NLT

When I was around the age of 7, my dad and I went squirrel hunting early one morning. We hurriedly got dressed and left without eating breakfast at home because my dad wanted to get us "big milk and a roll," aka a carton of chocolate milk and a cinnamon roll, from the gas station on our way to the woods, where we would be hunting. It was what we always did when we would go hunting. I was the apple of my dad's eye, his little buddy. I simply adored him and loved spending time alone with him doing whatever made him happy, which inadvertently was always doing something in nature. Spending time with him made me feel like I was the most important person in the world, so special. Some of my favorite times were with him. I do not recall the conversation we had leading up to this, but I distinctly remember him informing me, *"I always wanted a boy, but I got you."* Although I did not say anything in reply, those words unsettled me and replayed in my mind the rest of the day and throughout the rest of my life, up until now. I am certain my dad meant no harm by saying what he said, but the enemy used those words, and they became the second ember planted in my soul. The message I got from those words was that I was a disappointment, less than what was hoped for, and second rate. Since I was not the son he had hoped for, I felt like I had to earn his love and his attention. So, I learned how to hunt, fish, trap, shoot guns, make slingshots, gut squirrels and deer, build tree stands, and split firewood. As long as I was doing these things, my dad wanted to be around me. We had amazing times together, and he taught me so much. My love for nature came from him. For which I am forever grateful. Little did I know a lie, **I am a disappointment, less than hoped for**, what I will refer to as **Ember #2**, was placed and slowly burning through to the core of my being.

MY TRUTH: I am NOT a mistake, and my Heavenly Father delights in me!

"You made all the delicate, inner parts of my body and knit me together in my mother's womb. Thank you for making me so wonderfully complex! Your workmanship is marvelous - how well I know it. You watched me as I was being formed in utter seclusion, as I was woven together in the dark of the womb. You saw me before I was born. Every day of my life was recorded in your book. Every moment was laid out before a single day had passed. How precious are your thoughts about me, O God? I can't even count them; they outnumber the grains of sand! And when I wake up, you are still with me!" – Psalms 139:13-18 NLT

"For the LORD your God is living among you. He is a mighty savior. He will take delight in you with gladness. With his love, he will calm all your fears. He will rejoice over you with joyful songs." – Zephaniah 3:17 NLT

The Making of Embers #3 and #4

I will jump ahead to another pivotal time in my childhood. I was right at the age of 10 when I told my mom I wanted to get my ears pierced. She told me I had to ask my dad. *"If God wanted you to have holes in your ears, you would have been born with them."* Which irrevocably meant, *"NO!"* I really wanted them pierced, and I would not take *"No"* for an answer, so I kept begging mom to let me get them pierced. Finally, the day came. One Saturday, we went and had them done. I was so proud and could not wait to get home and show my dad, who I just knew would love how I looked. I could not have been more wrong! He was reading the local newspaper when mom and I got home. I stood in front of him and asked him if he noticed anything different? He saw them, put the newspaper up, and completely ignored me for weeks later. Here is where another lie was sown…that lie, **Ember #3; if you do something someone does not like, they will withdraw from you and stop loving you.** The truth is, he did not stop loving me, but it sure felt like it.

MY TRUTH: Nothing can separate (me) from the love of God in Christ Jesus. He will never leave me nor forsake me.

And I am convinced that nothing can ever separate us from God's love. Neither death nor life, neither angels nor demons,[u] neither our fears for today nor our worries about

tomorrow—not even the powers of hell can separate us from
God's love. – Romans 8:38 NLT

Don't love money; be satisfied with what you have. For God has
said, "I will never fail you. I will never abandon you." –
Hebrews 13:5 NLT

My dad was angry with me for several weeks after I had my ears pierced. After what felt like was FOREVER, my dad finally started talking with me again, and our outdoor adventures continued on the weekends up until I turned 12. On this particular day, we had been squirrel hunting and had come home to clean them so we could eat them for dinner. Something was very strange. I felt nauseous and eventually threw up at the sight of the blood and guts. I told dad, *"I just cannot do this anymore, Dad, the blood and guts make me sick."* He replied, *"What is wrong with you?!"* I was trying to explain to him that I had started my period, but he interrupted me and said, *"Oh, I see, you turned into a girl!"* Now, granted, I may have been a little emotional, but those words hit me like a ton of bricks! We never went hunting together again after that day. One thing was confirmed that day in my mind; Dad really did not want a girl. I was less than what he had hoped for. The lie planted that day was **Ember #4; I am not good enough to spend time with, because I am a girl.** I could not help but question in my heart, "Is there something wrong with me?"

MY TRUTH: I was created by God on purpose, for a purpose. In Him, I lack nothing!

"So, God created human beings in his own image. In the image of
God he created them; male and female he created them." –
Genesis 1:27 NLT

"For we are God's handiwork, created in Jesus Christ to do good works, which God prepared in advance for us to do." – Ephesians 2:10 NIV

"...' My grace is all you need. My power works best in weakness...'" – 2 Corinthians 12:9 NLT

The Making of Embers #5 and #6

Needless to say, my relationship with my dad was quite different after that. He started spending time with my little sister instead of me. Although it was hard for me to adjust, I finally came to grips with the fact that I had been replaced. I was so hurt at how quickly and easily I had been replaced. There you have it, the lie, **Ember #5, I am replaceable.** All the while, one ember piled upon another and continued to burn deeper and deeper into my core. I listened to the lies of the enemy and began to partner with them. It was not long after I started to really believe them. I kept all this to myself. Each time I rehearsed the lies in my mind, I breathed life into them, without being aware of it, and inadvertently added fuel to the fire.

My TRUTH: God wants to spend time alone with me. He considers me irreplaceable.

"...Rise up, my darling! Come away with me, my fair one." – Song of Solomon 2:10 NLT

Puberty set in early for me, unfortunately. I started developing much earlier than the other girls in my grade, which caused a real problem. I am not sure how gym class is in this day and age, but back then, we had to take communal showers after gym class. This was when I noticed there was something "wrong" with me. There you have it, another lie, **Ember #6, there is something innately wrong with me, and everyone knows it.** See, I had developed pubic hair, and no one else had any. Of course, now I know this is normal, but back then, there was nothing normal about it to me. I was already riddled with shame and guilt and had zero self-esteem; this was just the icing on the cake! I started avoiding the communal showers and started cleaning up in a bathroom stall after class, which caused speculation from some of the "mean girls." It was not long before the "mean girls" concluded I was in there stuffing my bra.

They started calling me Charmin. In their opinions, that was the logical reason for me not showering with the rest of the girls and the reason for me having breast before anyone else did. The girls told the boys. Soon everyone started calling me Charmin every chance they got. Even during the summer, I could not escape from their taunting words. I was in the girls' softball league and ended up playing against some of the "mean girls." When I would get up to bat, they would chant, *"Hey Charmin, Charmin... "* instead of *"Hey batter, batter..."* It was so embarrassing and demeaning. I recall my family and I were at the grocery store one Saturday morning, and mom asked me to carry out the toilet tissue, one of my LEAST favorite things to carry because of the harassment at school.

As luck would have it, when we walked out of the store, low and behold, yep, you guessed it…there was one of the mean girls coming in the store with her family. She saw me and laughed out loud. As we passed each other, she said, *"I knew it! Hi, Charmin."* This all sounds laughable now, but then, it was absolutely horrific. Kids can be cruel, and once you are labeled with a nickname, it sticks. I did not shake that nickname until my Junior year in High School. I finally found the courage to get out of the bathroom stall

and prove to them once and for all by lifting my shirt and my bra and saying right to their faces, *"Does this look like Charmin to you?"*

Let me just say, their eyes were bulging out of their heads, and they never called me that again, lol. I only wish I had the courage to do that years before.

My TRUTH: God considers me a masterpiece, which means I am treasured.

"For we are God's masterpiece. He has created us anew in Christ Jesus, so we can do the good things he planned for us long ago."
– Ephesians 2:10 NLT

"For the Lord, your God is living among you. He is a mighty savior. He will take delight in you with gladness. With his love, he will calm all your fears. He will rejoice over you with joyful songs." – Zephaniah 3:17 NLT

With what lies have you partnered? If you are like me, you can instantly recall when words were spoken over you that made you feel less than. I challenge you to pause for a moment and write them down.

What was spoken over you that pierced your soul? How old were you? Who said it? How did it make you feel? How has believing those words charted your course?

_____

_____

_____

_____

_____

_____

_____

_____

_____

Contrast those lies with TRUTH. Which Truth will you proclaim over yourself?

_____

_____

_____

_____

_____

_____

_____

_____

_____

_____

_____

_____

Innocence lost

My family was very active in a small country church, where I met a handsome boy who started showing me attention, something that I desperately craved. He asked me to be his girlfriend, and it was not long after that, I lost my virginity at the tender age of 14 to, Nathan, my first love. I just KNEW we were going to get married, so I justified giving myself to him. He was only 15. At the age of 14, I had my entire future planned out in my head.

I believed I would have three children, a beautiful home with the proverbial white picket fence, a college education, a great career, and I would live happily ever after. That was my dream, and I expected my life to turn out just like that. No one could tell me it would be any different. We were way too young to be having sex and talking about marriage, but you could not have convinced us of that. Looking back, I now know, when you awaken those sexual senses before their time, you open yourself up to a whole lot of pain.

About six months after we had sex, Nathan ended up having sex with another girl and broke my heart. How could I ever trust him again? Although I broke up with him, I felt like I been the one who had been broken up with. How could he have cheated on me? Anytime he wanted sex, and every time we were together, I gave it to him. I was devastated. I asked him how he could have done that to me? To which he replied, *"She knows more than you."* I took that to mean I was not good enough reinforcing the lie, Ember #5, and set me on a course of unprecedented poor choices and pain. In retrospect, in some regards, that statement set me on a quest to become more educated and better at it, so that would not happen to me again. Not a smart idea.

Desperately Seeking Love

I was so depressed I decided the best way to get over my boyfriend was to find another one…I know…I know…sounds like a bad idea. Yet, I was determined. My dad told me he never really cared for my first boyfriend because he was not a hunter. This time, I was on the prowl for a boy who liked to hunt. I was a sophomore in high school, helping the Yearbook committee sift through numerous photos to put in the yearbook, when I stumbled upon a photo of a boy, wearing a flannel shirt and jeans, posing with a buck he had killed. I was so excited! I had to find out who this boy was and get to know him. I started asking older kids in the class if they knew who he was and sure enough, someone did.

His name was Todd. Instead of just going up to him and introducing myself, I decided I would start wearing my flannels, jeans, and hiking boots to school and make sure I passed by the senior lockers, where he often hung out, hoping he would see me. I made sure he saw me. Soon after, we started dating. I invited him over, anxious for him to meet my dad. I just KNEW they would hit it off. I was right! Things were off to a good start.

He asked me to be his date for his senior prom. I was on Cloud 9! Things suddenly took a turn for the worse, though. On prom night, Todd was very persistent and ended up having his way with me. It was not an enjoyable experience. I felt so ashamed and cried until it was over. He told me I was lucky he even wanted to have anything to do with me. *"Who would want to have sex with someone like you, look at you! You are fat and ugly"*, he said. Weeks before I had told him I was not a virgin, something I should have kept to myself. Since he had been over to the house several times, he knew my parents were Christians and threatened to tell them how big a whore I was if I did not keep dating him. I know what you are thinking…BIG RED FLAG! I could not see it then. At that time in my life, I feared my parents more than God! I lacked confidence in myself and was so afraid of losing their love. Choosing what I thought was the lesser of two evils, I dated him for two years before getting engaged. Yes, I accepted his proposal. Fear of rejection causes you to make crazy choices!

For Better or Worse, Huh?

I graduated mid-term from my high school five months before commencement and started community college. Six months into my first year of college, I found out I was pregnant at the age of 17, just three months before my 18th birthday and wedding. It was only by the grace of God I did not get pregnant before then! Sharing this news with my parents was one of the hardest things I ever had to do. I knew they would be disappointed in me and shocked. They were, rightfully so. After all, they thought I was a good girl. Sadly, I was far from it.

Soon they accepted the fact that their teenage daughter was going to be a mother and supported me throughout my pregnancy. I gave birth to a healthy baby boy in March of 1989. Life, at that moment, was perfect for me. I was so in love with my son. I had never known the depths of love a heart could hold until I laid eyes on him. Being a mother was the greatest joy I had ever known! My entire world revolved around my son, and nothing else mattered; I mean NOTHING, not even my husband.

A week after my son was born, Todd had indicated on numerous occasions that he wanted to be intimate. As I said before, NOTHING else mattered to me but my son, so I would quickly dismiss his advances and told him I had not yet healed enough to have intercourse. I successfully put him off for 3 ½ months, but the day came when he would no longer take no for an answer. That day just happened to be the day my sister came to help me.

My sister, who is four years younger than me, came to spend time with my son and me during the summer. What a huge help she was, as I was still trying to perfect breastfeeding and had not yet figured out how to balance cooking, cleaning, and taking care of my newborn. I was so thankful she came. Sadly, things took a serious turn for the worse. I can remember that day as if it were just yesterday. I was sitting in a chair, breastfeeding my son. My sister was seated on the couch across from me when Todd came home from work, walked through the door, and saw my son nursing. This infuriated him, and he lost it! His face was red with anger, and his eyes were full of rage when he shouted, *"I am sick of him getting all your attention!"* After which, Todd ripped my son off my breast and tossed my baby onto the couch, grabbed me by the hair and dragged me down the hallway to the bedroom, where he stripped off my clothes, while I tried to fight him, screaming.

My sister consoles my crying son and places him in his crib, then comes into the room. In a panic at what she sees, she commences to wrap her arms around his neck and tries with all her might to get him off me. They struggle, yet Todd was determined to finish what he set out to do. My sister goes to the phone on a table in the bedroom and calls my dad to tell him that my husband was hurting me; undoubtedly, he could hear the struggle going on. Dad replied, *"What happens between them in that house is between them,"* and he hung up. My sister looks at me with tears running down her face. Feeling hopeless, the look of despair is all over her face, and fear is in her eyes. At that moment, something inside me died. I realized my dad would not come to my rescue, and this was really happening. My sister tried again to pull him off me. I stopped struggling for her sake. I could not stand the fear in her eyes.

Todd grabbed her and threw her out into the hallway, locked the door, then continued his agenda. I remember lying there, crying at first, then going somewhere else in my mind as he finished, saying to myself, *"This is not love. What is happening to me is not making love!"* I felt so violated, so vulnerable, so ashamed that my 14-year-old sister saw what she saw! I felt so powerless and so unloved, so used, so alone. He walked out and did not come home for two days. There I was, sobbing uncontrollably, not only for myself but also for my sister, whose innocence was lost. My life changed that day; life as I knew it was over. After Todd left, my sister and I did not talk about it. Avoidance seemed easier than trying to make sense of what had just happened. I just picked up my baby, loved on him, and tried to put all of this out of my head. Imagine my despair when I discovered I was…yep, you guessed it…pregnant with my second child!

To say I was mad at my husband, and God would be a gross understatement. I was devastated. This is NOT the way a child should be brought into the world!

Nonetheless, despite the fact I was not emotionally prepared for another child, my daughter was growing inside me. I remember crying out to God, telling him I did not want a child who was conceived in the manner she was conceived. It was not until I was eight months along that I finally accepted the fact that I had a child, and she deserved to feel wanted and loved. None of this was HER fault. I am so thankful for God's grace. It is the only way that I was able to accept this pregnancy and not hold anger and bitterness in my heart towards my dad or my husband. Sadly, nothing was ever the same between my dad and me or Todd and me.

My beautiful daughter was born in April 1990. Once again, my heart burst open with love. I fell in love with her the moment I heard her dainty little cry. She weighed 10 lbs. 9 oz and was over 3 lbs. larger than any other baby in the nursery, so her dainty little cry surprised me and captivated my heart. She was simply perfect in every way, a true blessing from God.

So, at the age of 19, I have a 13-month-old, a newborn, and a marriage on the rocks. I forgave my husband as much as I could at the time, even though he never apologized. Truthfully, I never forgot what happened that day in July. I graduated from community college just three days after my daughter was born. I swore to myself life would get better. I would do everything in my power to make myself better. Intimacy between my husband and I was strained, and at times I was forced to perform acts that I did not want to perform. The counsel I had received was, *"the marriage bed is not defiled...and it is your duty as a wife to do whatever your husband asks you to do."*

He would use anal sex as punishment and forced me to perform oral sex on him as control. I tried to get on the pill because I did not want to have another child in this marriage. Apparently, he desired to keep me barefoot and pregnant and trapped forever.

He started hiding my birth control pills and played mind games. He would take my wedding ring off my finger while I was asleep and would hide it then wake me up to accuse me of leaving it on a nightstand at some other man's home. Of course, that was not the truth. Todd could sense me pulling away, and the abuse escalated. Feeling trapped in my circumstance and striving to change whatever I could to make myself feel better, I joined Weight Watchers and lost 90 pounds, then found out I was pregnant yet again. This time, the news was not as devastating as before. I had already determined in my mind that my marriage was going to be over. I knew a line had been crossed, and there was no coming back from it. This remained a secret throughout the entire pregnancy. I had to plan my escape, somehow.

In September, just 20 days after my 21st birthday, my youngest daughter was born. My heart, again, burst open with boundless love for her. My love for Todd, on the other hand, became non-existent. Where love once resided, resentment dwelled. The level of strain and tension only escalated during the following year and a half. I endured repeated sexual abuse and felt I had been reduced to a mere shell of who I was intended to be; I was so unhappy, unfulfilled, felt so unloved, so used, and abused. As a result of one episode of sexual abuse, I sought medical attention for anal bleeding that had continued for three weeks. It took such courage for me to even go to the doctor. Remember, I was told that whatever happens in the marriage bed is undefiled; therefore, what I was going through was supposed to be "normal." Yet, EVERYTHING inside was screaming for HELP!

I never told the doctor WHAT had happened to me; I only explained the symptoms. No questions were ever asked, none whatsoever. Oh, how I wish that the nurse or doctor had asked me, *"Have you been assaulted?"* or *"What happened?"* Sadly, that never happened. The doctor casually dismissed me and told me the bleeding should stop on it its own in a couple of days. *What?! That's it?* I felt so hopeless while I was getting dressed. I remember going out to the car and crying my eyes out, wondering why no one could see me, the pain I was in, the horrible marriage I was in…why no one took the time to ask important questions? Could this actually be "normal?" Again, EVERYTHING inside me screamed, "THERE IS NOTHING NORMAL ABOUT WHAT I AM GOING THROUGH!!!"

Desperately Seeking a Way Out!

Beside myself, I cried until I was about a mile away from home and had to shut it off. I could not let my babies see me like this. I could not risk Todd knowing how broken I was, I reasoned. So, I once again put on the "mask" I was so accustomed to wearing and continued just to exist and go through the motions. After each episode of abuse, my husband would send me flowers at work. The ladies at work were oblivious to what I was going through, so they just could not comprehend how I could throw them in the trash the moment they arrived. No one knew the pain I was in or would believe the abuse I was going through.

I dreaded going home every day. I could not wait to get home to see my babies, but I did not want to be around my husband. My parents did not believe in divorce, under any circumstance, so I was stuck. I could not get anyone to listen to me or see the pain behind my smile. My disdain for him was so strong that even the smell of his clean body would make me vomit, literally. Vulnerable, broken, desperate, and dying inside, I looked outside my marriage for solace from Malcolm, one of the men from my church, who was 19 years older than me, thinking he would give me the fatherly advice and love I was craving. Unfortunately, advice and fatherly love was not the only thing he was willing to give me. Soon after, we had an affair.

Finally, I had someone who would comfort me and agree that what was happening to me was abuse and not normal. Hear me! I am in no way saying the affair was the right choice. Being heard and understood was such a beautiful thing, though; it empowered me and gave me hope. Unfortunately, it was twisted and not, at all, the right thing to do. The sex we had was consensual, a welcome contrast to what I had at home. I started standing up for myself in my marriage, which only escalated things to the point of having a

shotgun pointed at my head while I was lying in bed with my 3-year-old daughter on one occasion.

On another occasion, I had a knife held to my throat, with all three of my children crying and pleading for their daddy to stop hurting me. The morning after the knife incident was the day I finally had enough. I remember that morning very well. I was folding laundry while sitting on the couch, when my son, who was 4 ½, declared out of the clear blue, *"When I grow up I am going to be just like my Daddy!"* The very thought of my sweet, beautiful boy growing up to be like his Dad made my blood run cold. I called my mom and asked if the kids and I could move in with her and dad because I was going to file for divorce. She told me she could not let me do that because they did not believe in divorce. I called Malcolm and asked him if we could move in with him. He agreed, so I scheduled an appointment with an attorney and filed for divorce.

With the divorce pending, the kids and I moved out of the house and moved into my lover's house. This arrangement, of course, did not please my parents whatsoever. I felt like I was between a rock and a hard place…where else was I supposed to go? I was unemployed and destitute at that time, and my parents would not let me move in with them. I do not regret divorcing Todd; it truly was a matter of survival. At least now, I was safe.

Some VERY important lessons I learned from this divorce were:
You should NEVER seek advice or comfort from the opposite sex when you are in a vulnerable state of mind. When you are vulnerable, you are easily taken advantage of.
People of both sexes will say exactly what they think you want to hear often because they have an agenda.

- I should have gone to a professional counselor. It would have been a much different outcome for me had I done so. I cannot stress the importance of being heard without fear of rejection or reprisal.
- A mate does not complete you; only God does.
- If an intimate act is forced upon you, it is not love.
- If you make choices out of fear or despair, you are not thinking rationally.
- If your gut is telling you something is not right, not normal...LISTEN!
- Sometimes you must make tough decisions, and not everyone is going to like them. You will have to deal with the consequences. When you finally get sick and tired of being sick and tired, you will do something about your situation; you will not worry about what other people think.

Todd had my van repossessed shortly after the divorce. I had no way to get to work if I wanted to and had no support system. I felt like I could not go to church anymore because, after all, I was an adulteress woman! I exchanged one form of hell for another one! I gained over 100 pounds and tried to make the most of my new life. I made my bed, so I had to lay in it, right? Let me stop here for just a moment and clarify something. If ANYONE is telling you, "You made your bed, now lay in it," I want to encourage you. There is NO mistake too big for God to forgive. God does not think those thoughts towards you.

From the Frying Pan into the Fire

A year after my divorce was finalized, Malcolm and I got married, with only two witnesses and the minister at our ceremony. My parents hated him and had very little to do with me after I left my first husband. They sided with my ex because they felt I had wronged him by having an affair. Yes, I did wrong him by having an affair. I do not deny that. However, two wrongs NEVER make a right. There is something called Cause and Effect at play here. Had I not gone through the abuse I would not have contemplated having an affair in the first place. Let me make this perfectly clear… abuse is NEVER ok and having an affair is NEVER ok. I am not justifying either.

We moved into a bigger place out in the country, and things started to settle down a bit. Malcolm bought me a new car for my birthday, and I was able to get employment. Money was still tight, though, because Todd stopped paying child support. Because it was $7,000 in arrears, I took him to court, thinking the court would be on my side. Ha…that was wishful thinking. Instead, the judge cut his arrearage in half, LOWERED his weekly child support, and basically slapped him on the wrist. After the court hearing, Todd decided to stop seeing the kids every other week. Once again, he stopped paying support, thinking his decision justified him not paying support. It sucks when your ex does not pay support because the kids are the ones who end up suffering. I could not get him to understand that.

Sadly, it did not take very long for Malcolm to reveal his true colors. He enjoyed the chase but was not interested in marriage, or the commitment required to support a family of 5. Once we were married, he became so controlling. He did not want me to see my family at all. Ok…I get it…they did not like him. He felt I was disrespecting him by wanting to be with people who hated him so much. Despite their disapproval of my marriage, I know they truly loved me and longed for me to be in their life.

When I would go to visit them, Malcolm would treat me horribly when I got home. I was cut to my core with his words of contempt for me. I believe he was trying to make me leave, although he never said he wanted a divorce. He went as far as to limit the squares of toilet tissue I used. I kid you not! You may be asking yourself, *"Why in the world would she allow him to have that kind of control?"* That is a fair question. I will do my best to help you understand the frame of mind I was in at that time in hopes that it will shed some light on my reasoning. I was so broken and confused, had no self-esteem whatsoever, and did not know my worth! When a woman does not know who she is or her worth, she will allow all sorts of abuse and neglect; she will not only make excuses for the perpetrator/abuser, but she will convince herself and try to convince you that she was at fault, or she deserved it. It is a sad reality of a broken woman.

Words of Hope

This is just ONE of the many reasons I am sharing my story. There are countless women and truthfully some men out there that need someone to HEAR what they are not saying and see the pain behind their smiles. There are people out there who need to know they are precious in the sight of God. They are loved beyond belief, even though no one else has shown them love. They need someone to tell them the abuse is NEVER ok. They need someone to tell them they are priceless! Most importantly, they need someone to tell them there is no mistake too big that God cannot turn around for their good. If that is you, let me pause for a moment and ask you to repeat these words after me:

"I am precious in the sight of God."
"I am loved beyond belief."
"I deserve to be treasured."
"I am worthy of love."

"I am worthy of respect."
"I am priceless."
"I am greater than other's opinions of me."
"I am more than the sum of my past mistakes."

It took me over 30 years to FINALLY get this! I wish someone had said those words to me. These words are filled with hope and life. Repeat them out loud as often as you need to until you believe them! How you think about yourself, and the words that you profess out loud about yourself are very powerful. No matter what you have been through, there are brighter days ahead; trust me.

The Darkness Before the Dawn

Sadly, matters only got worse. Malcolm started entertaining pornography and would openly leave his magazines out on the bed for me to see. He knew I hated pornography, but he did not care. He wanted me to know that I did not look like any of those women. He stopped having sex with me and would call me names. The things that would come out of his mouth sounded like things straight from the pit of hell, so vile and mean. It was a living hell for me, one that I had created myself. This time, however, I had support from my mom and my dad because they hated him from the beginning. I was trying so hard to make the marriage work. I could not bear the thought of having a 2nd failed marriage.

When Malcolm was away at work, I would invite my mom over to pray with me over the house. We prayed that the peace of God would fill our home and that if my husband could not say something nice that he would keep his mouth shut. There was peace in the house until he walked through the door. It felt as if he brought a legion of demons in with him. The house would feel so dark, and the air would feel thick with hate.

The kids and I started going to church regularly again as a reprieve from the chaos. I prayed countless prayers for my marriage, but nothing seemed to change. In my attempt to make our marriage work, I asked one of the young girls I knew from the church if she would be willing to stay the night to watch the kids so that Malcolm and I could go out on a date. She agreed, and I was hopeful. He and I had a nice evening. He was full of smiles and flirtatious, more like the man I fell in love with. However, my hopes were completely shattered when we returned later that evening. The sitter and the kids were fast asleep. We quietly turned in for bed, and he initiated foreplay. It was the first time in several months. Naked and passionately entwined, Malcolm whispered in my ear and asked me if I would ask the 14-year old babysitter if she would join us in the bedroom. He told me all evening he had been fantasizing about that. Now I knew the reason for his smiles and flirtatious behavior during dinner. I was APPALLED and said, *"ABSOLUTELY NOT!* I quickly got dressed, woke her, and drove her home. HOW COULD THIS BE HAPPENING?!

My troubles only increased after that night. Malcolm started torturing me mentally. He would say things like:

"I am going to burn the house down with you and the kids in it; if I were you, I would not sleep too soundly."

"You should always make sure you check the car before you drive it. You never know if I have cut the gas line or the brakes."

"I am surprised you made it home. I put an open can of gasoline in the trunk of the car, hoping it would spill out and drip onto the tailpipe and catch the car on fire with you in it!"

I cannot begin to tell you the emotional torment I was under while married to this man. This time instead of trying to find solace from another man, I started seeking God like never before.

I love you so.
Fall in love with me,
Fall in love with me.
Let me hold you in my arms
Keep you safe from harm.
I love you so."

I have not heard of many people who can say they have had God sing over them, but it happened to me. You would think that would be enough to cause me to stop seeking love and affection from men, but that was not what happened.

Premarital Sex in the Projects

I started taking care of myself, and with the stress now eliminated, I was able to lose weight again. I kept praying for God to send me someone to share life with. Although most would have called it quits after two failed marriages, I kept believing that one day I would have my happily ever after. Towards the end of our year in the projects, I was introduced to Michael, a widower. Because he came highly recommended by a couple, I knew from church, and I agreed to allow them to give him my phone number. We talked for hours, day after day. Soon we met, and the kids loved him from the very moment they met him. Since I had never dealt with my issues, I still had a warped sense of what love is. Equating sex with love, I gave myself to him almost immediately. After a short time of dating, Michael asked my mom and dad if he could have my hand in marriage, asked me to be his wife, and I said, *"Yes!"*

We were married in a small church that was filled with our closest friends and family. My Dad asked me before he walked me down the aisle if I was sure about this and I told him I had never been so sure in all my life. I meant that with my whole heart. Michael adopted my three kids. My happily ever after had finally started! Life has a funny way of dashing dreams sometimes. Michael, employed by a local logging company, had a horrific logging accident, shortly after we were married. Someone had cut some treetops but had not felled them properly.

Walking through the logging site, he heard a whistling sound; he turned to look over his shoulder, and a huge tree fell on his shoulder, plowing him into the wet forest floor. His shoulder, back, and tibia were broken. He was rushed to the hospital and laid there in excruciating pain for hours. I arrived at the hospital but was not permitted to see him, for what felt like forever. When I finally had the opportunity to see Michael, I was sickened by his injuries and nearly fainted. He was lucky there had been a wet forest floor, according to the doctor. Had it not rained three days straight before the incident, he would have been dead.

I am 27 years old at this time, in my 3rd marriage, with a husband who is critically injured and unable to work for an indefinite amount of time. I had to pick up two part-time jobs on top of my full-time job to make ends meet. This was a level of stress I had never experienced before. There are no words to tell you how emotionally and physically draining this time of my life was. Thankfully, he finally was able to come home. Our community helped us out tremendously by building a wheelchair ramp and took up a collection of food and supplied us with meals. Again, God provided. I had to arrange for a hospital bed and a portable potty to be put into the house. He was confined to that hospital bed for seven months. I had to clean the external fixator screwed into his knee and ankle several times a day, wipe him, and give him sponge baths on top of working three jobs and maintaining the household. I was off one day a month and literally would sleep the entire day.

Yet, I remained hope-filled and trusted God to make sense of all this somehow. Michael was in a great deal of pain every day and was tormented daily by feelings of worthlessness since he could not work and take care of the family or himself. He became severely depressed and very bitter. To deal with it, I absorbed myself in ministry and church activities six days a week.

Fuel to the Fire

Months slowly pass, and eventually, my husband is able to get around with the aid of a cane. I was hopeful things would start to get back to normal again. Due to the nature of Michael's injuries, we were not able to be intimate. Unfortunately, even long after he was able to move around again, his "equipment" just would not work. This was extremely difficult for both of us. At night, he would go on the computer and would indulge in porn while I lay in bed asleep, although I was not aware of it at the time. Countless times I was awakened by him masturbating beside me. Instead of addressing it, I just lay there in the dark, with my back to him, with tears running down my face night after night. The embers of my formative years became full flames, reinforced each time it happened. Finally, one day I mustered up the courage and asked him why he would do that when I was lying there and longing for him to make love to me. He never answered. His silence was screaming, "YOU'RE NOT ENOUGH!"

With each passing day, Michael's anger grew. It became unbearable. I confided in my mom, my sounding board; we talked for hours every day. I became emotionally dependent on her...I will confess I was co-dependent. She always made me feel better. I took his anger very personally and was unable to see how badly he was hurting on the inside. I wish I could say things miraculously turned around for good, but that would be a lie. Instead, after

Michael gained full mobility, the unthinkable happened! He started molesting my girls, unbeknownst to me until a year after it had stopped. Sundays, literally EVERY Sunday, there was turmoil in the house.

It came to the point that I dreaded Sundays because he was always so angry. He would yell at the kids and me all the way to church. Little did I know it was his guilt eating him alive. I would send him upstairs to wake the kids up each Sunday morning, while I made breakfast. That was when he would fondle them. My oldest daughter started being extremely defiant and mouthy towards me and even started sleeping fully clothed. I asked her why she was doing that? She just said, *"So I do not have to get up earlier in the mornings."* Little did I know she was doing it to keep Michael from fondling her. Imagine the guilt I felt after I learned this was happening! After all, I was the one that asked him to go up there every Sunday morning! How could this happen under my roof while I am in the house, and I did not know it?! Believe me it can, it did!

The Secret is Out!

I am so proud of my girls for finding the courage to tell a family friend who told my mom, who told me. I am not kidding, the moment I found out I felt all five stages of grief all at once! Needing to confirm for myself, I went to the family friend and asked her to tell me what she had been told. Then I went to my daughters and asked them to tell me what happened. My heart broke for them, and my life again was in ruins around me. Life as I knew it ended that day. I did not know what to do, but I knew I needed to do something. I went directly to my Pastor. He told me, *"If you do not call the police, I will. I will give you one hour."* I left the church and went to the police station to file a report. My children were at their biological grandmother's house for the weekend, and I asked my parents if I could stay with them.

I chose not to confront Michael about the allegations. Instead, the police came and arrested him. The next morning an arrest record was posted in the local paper. Although it did not list my girls' names, everyone in the small town knew who they were, and news spread quickly, as it always does in small towns. Once again, I was faced with shame and guilt.

Depression Sets In

The stress of all this was so overwhelming that I ended up having a migraine for 13 days straight. I was so depressed. Finally, I could not take it anymore. I sought medical attention from the small-town doctor, whose office was directly across the street from my house. The doctor told me I had situational depression and prescribed medication. I also sought out counseling for the girls and me. They did not want to go, but I felt it was so important for them to have someone to talk with. For me, counseling was crucial. I dare not even begin to know how I would have made it through that ordeal without it! The counseling center I went through was a faith-based center run by one of the ladies from my church. It offered para-professional counseling at no cost, which was a Godsend, considering I was struggling to make ends meet.

It was during these counseling sessions that I started to discover the lies that I had believed, the deep emotional scars I was carrying, and found the emotional healing I desperately needed. I will forever be grateful for my sweet counselor, Katy. She prayed with me each week, and most importantly, she prayed *for* me between our sessions. I went through a divorce recovery program and started making sense of everything.

Michael was released on bond while the case was pending and stayed with his parents in a small town about 20 minutes away from our house. My counselor suggested I schedule a meeting with him face to face and asked him if what the girls said was true? He admitted he had fondled them but stressed he had never penetrated either of them in any way. He showed remorse, but I felt like he was only sorry because he had been caught! The abuse had stopped a year prior, just like the girls had said, but I still could not trust him. Besides, the state had already taken the case...so it was out of my hands. I insisted that he get counseling. I wanted to get to the bottom of this! I wanted to know WHY this happened, HOW this happened, and WHERE we go from here.

Grace Covered Me

I was so angry! The fact that it happened infuriated me! I had to have some answers. One day I was alone at the house. I cannot remember where the kids were, but I was in the bedroom on my knees, crying out to God. In gut-wrenching honesty, I poured out my heart, my anger, my disappointment, my grief, and my tears. I am not sure how long I was there, but I know I had exhausted myself. I asked God how he could expect me to forgive Michael for doing such a thing to my girls? It was at that moment; I heard the still small voice of God, ask me, *"Do you think your sins were any less? Have you not been forgiven much?"* Knowing what I had done in my past, I knew my sins were just as vile as his. I also knew I had been forgiven for some pretty unspeakable things. Looking up with my eyes open, tears streaming down my face, and in complete surrender, all I could do was ask God, *"Lord, please help me be willing to be willing to forgive him."* God heard me and answered me in a miraculous way! I felt like a ton of bricks had been lifted off my shoulders, and I suddenly felt a warm to the bone sensation like warm oil being poured over my head and covering me. It was an incredible, life-changing experience. God revealed to me that this was His grace and reminded me that it is sufficient.

"...he said, 'My grace is all you need. My power works best in weakness...'" – 2 Corinthians 12:9 NLT

Not fully understanding all that had happened, I started looking into what Grace means. The Funk & Wagnall dictionary defines grace as:

- Beauty or harmony of motion, form, or manner
- Service freely rendered
- The act of showing favor
- Clemency, mercy
- The love of God toward man
- The divine influence operating in man
- The state of being pleasing to God
- Any divinely inspired spiritual virtue or excellence to God

This day I found out grace is so much more than amazing, like the old hymn declares. It truly is a tangible thing. To simplify it a bit, I discovered God's grace gave me divine empowerment to do what otherwise I could never do. Before that moment, I had felt completely powerless and devastated, but when His grace covered me, I felt light as a feather, strong as an ox, and confident

He would be with me and help me get through this. After much prayer, I concluded that I would not divorce Michael but try to work through all of it. I know many of you will sense your blood beginning to boil as a result of my decision. My parents felt the same way. Believe me, this was not the easy route! It would have been much easier just to walk away, but that was not what I felt God was asking me to do. I do not expect you to understand. Please continue reading. I think you will be shocked at how things turned out.

Piranha Christians

The Pastor disagreed with my decision and immediately removed me from all my church roles, and my kids were no longer able to help with Children's Church, the Nursery, or serve in any capacity. I was told I had to take a year off from my responsibilities because parishioners were threatening to stop coming to the church or, at the very least, stop financially supporting the church. The Pastor did what he felt was the only logical thing to do. Although having all that stripped away from me at that time was embarrassing and painful, it truthfully was best. I needed time to process all that was happening and be there for my kids. Church members were encouraged to ostracize me and told not to console me if they saw me crying. It was during this time when I lost family, friends, and my ministry, I found out that Jesus truly is a friend that is closer than a brother, and He never leaves or forsakes you.

"...but a real friend sticks closer than a brother." – Proverbs 18:24 NLT

"...I will never fail you. I will never abandon you." – Hebrews 13:5 NLT

Michael's day of reckoning came, and he was pronounced guilty as charged and had to serve time in the county jail. I had no other choice but to work three jobs again to pay the bills. I continued my emotional healing and grew in my faith exponentially. The ladies at the counseling center were so surprised at my progress they asked me if I would be willing to take the para-professional counselor training myself. I did, and even MORE, emotional healing came my way. I am so thankful for all I learned from the Center for Women's Ministries. Layer upon layer of pain was peeled away, and I saw things completely different. See, before, I had processed my entire life through the eyes of a wounded little girl. In many ways, my emotional health had been stunted, so it was no wonder I had made some of the poor choices I had made. My first emotionally traumatizing experience happened when I was four years old. In essence, I was processing life at the emotional age of 4, although I did not know it.

The training I received help me to understand the lies I believed had charted a course of impending destruction for me. Those lies, like embers, that were placed in my soul, had silently become full-fledged flames, and now my life was in charred ruins around me. Yet, I remained hopeful. My faith was stretched beyond belief. Believe me, the choice to stay married to my husband was, up to that point, the hardest choice I had ever made. While Michael was incarcerated, I continued to receive emotional healing and gained more understanding. Each passing week, my faith increased, and my love and adoration for God did too.

Please hear me...there cannot be enough said about the need and importance of getting to the core issues and facing them head-on. If you have found yourself in a perpetual cycle that you just cannot seem to escape, there is a reason. More importantly, there is hope! You CAN break the cycle and experience joy. You just need to be willing to expose what has been hidden, stop seeing yourself as a victim, and start taking ownership of your choices. You do have a say in how your life will turn out. You may not be able to change the past, but you can change the way you look at it. You can also choose to live life with the understanding that life is not happening *to* you; it is happening *through* you.

During this difficult time of my life, God directed me to a song that reflected the declaration of my heart. If you have never heard the song, "Praise You in This Storm," a song by Casting Crowns, I invite you to stop whatever you are doing and listen to it. This song seemed to encapsulate the cry of my heart. It does not matter what "storm" you are in; you can resolve to praise God through it.

Time Served

Time passed, Michael completed his sentence and probation and gradually moved back into the house with the children and me. Not long after that, my son went off to the Marine Corps, my oldest daughter graduated, and her boyfriend moved in with us, and my youngest daughter told us she was pregnant. I thought we were going to have some form of normalcy again. All this happened so quickly I felt like my head would spin.

The good thing was my girls were rebuilding their trust and relationship with their dad, and I believed we were on the right path to becoming whole, but that is not what happened. After all, we had been through together, Michael concluded he no longer wanted to be married to me; he filed for divorce. To say I was shocked is a gross understatement! There was a temptation to become bitter towards him. After all, I stuck by his side through all of this when most women would have had him castrated. He told me he wanted me to move out. I had to make plans to find another place to stay.

I could not believe after all we had been through, he could just throw me away. It felt like a slap in the face, especially since I had lost so much—friends, family, my ministry, my church. My faith was shattered! Despite all God had revealed to me and the deep relationship I had cultivated with him during the latter part of my marriage, I started to doubt God's love for me once again. How could He do this to me or allow this to happen? I did everything He asked me to. Now I had nothing. There I was, covered in the soot of the charred ruins of my life!

Valuable Lessons I learned from this marriage:

- 🕊 Two broken people do not make a whole.
- 🕊 Nothing can stay hidden; the truth will be revealed eventually, and you will have to face the facts.
- 🕊 Brokenness and unresolved traumas will come back to haunt you.
- 🕊 Once you become married, you are to leave your mother and father and cleave to your spouse.
- 🕊 Ministry and being involved with the church are great, but there needs to be a balance. Too much of anything is a gateway for problems.

Divine Intervention

I asked Gary, a friend of mine, if I could stay at his place for a little while until I could get a place of my own. He said, *"Yes."* Since I did not contest the divorce and because our kids were grown, the divorce was finalized in no time. I packed up my clothes and some home décor items and moved in with my friend in a tiny one-bedroom apartment. I slept on the couch for a short while, but it was not long before we were sleeping together. You would have thought I would have learned my lesson from before, but even after all I had learned at the Center for Women's Ministry, I still felt like I had to have a man to be complete.

We had so much fun together. We connected on so many levels that before long, I fell in love with him. There was a 14-year age difference between us, but that did not matter. Some may say I was going through a midlife crisis…maybe I was; I am not sure. I felt alive and carefree with him. We went on fishing trips, took road trips, and stayed up all hours of the night talking, watching movies, and listening to music. I started to enjoy this newfound freedom a little too much. He exposed me to weed, and we smoked it regularly, something I NEVER thought I would ever do. The Bible says, "There is pleasure in sin for a season…" but then there are consequences. God stepped in and did a divine intervention. In less than a month, he got arrested for failing a sobriety test. He revoked his probation and was sent to prison. I took over Gary's apartment while he was gone, and my youngest daughter moved in with me. I went to visit him once a week and sent him money for commissary for a year and a half during his incarceration. We wrote letters to each other every day, and since the church no longer wanted anything to do with me, I devoted all my free time to him. Looking back, I realize how ridiculous it was. The heart wants what it wants, right? I should have left well enough alone, but I did not. I was loyal to a fault. I stayed committed to him and supported him emotionally and financially. I closed down his apartment and rented an apartment for my daughter, first grandchild, and myself.

Danger Ahead

One night, my neighbors asked me to visit. Little did I know they had invited a friend of theirs over for me to meet; they were not aware I was in love with someone else. The separation was starting to take its toll, and I was finding it difficult to maintain a relationship with a man in prison. My neighbors introduced me to their friend, Tim, and we hit it off right away. I found this man to be interesting, intelligent, charming, and a joy to be around. He was a retired Marine veteran and had earned four master's degrees. I learned he was also a former minister and had written and published books. I was impressed, to say the least.

We started dating, and within a couple of months, he proposed. It felt so good to be wanted. I accepted his proposal, moved out of the apartment, and into a townhouse that he and I leased. Tim had some issues, but I felt I could manage them. He had one leg amputated as a result of a bomb that exploded while he was in service. He had PTSD and diabetes, so he was on some heavy-duty meds, like Fentanyl patches and OxyContin. However, there were times he would be so out of it that he would drool and slur his words. After he would snap out of it, sometimes hours later, he would tell me his sugar had dropped. I was so naïve! Truly, a more accurate way to say it is I was so stupid! I believed him. I felt pity for him and thought he needed me. The reality is he was a drug addict.

Tim did not come home the night before the wedding. He had told me he was going to go out with his friends for his bachelor party, so I did not think that to be strange. Our ceremony was to be held in our townhouse in the intimate company of some of our closest friends and loved ones. I had so much to do to get ready for the ceremony. The morning of the wedding, Tim came through the door and appeared to be having one of his "spells." Being sincerely concerned, I called his best man and asked for him to come over to help me access the situation because he was worse than I had ever seen him. He came over and pulled me to the side to tell me Tim was not going to snap out of it before the ceremony. I found out that he had NOT been with his friends but had instead been at the casino gambling all night. How he made it home is beyond me. He had overdosed on pills and had cut open his patches, covered a knife with the fentanyl, heated it with a lighter and burned it into his side, multiple times, which should have killed him!

I am in panic mode…when the pastor arrived at the house, I asked to speak to him in private in the upstairs bedroom. *"I cannot marry him like this,"* I insisted with tears running down my face. The Pastor looked me straight in the eye and said, *"Now, listen, you have already given yourself to him sexually, have you not?"* To which I replied, *"Yes."* He said, *"Then you are already married to him in God's eyes. You cannot abandon him now when he needs you the most!"* Those words hit me like a ton of bricks! The Pastor went out of the room and had Tim's mom come in to talk with me. She laid more guilt on my shoulders by telling me how I was supposed to be Tim's angel. Once again, I found myself trapped by a stupid choice I made.

The wedding went on, with Tim being physically held up by his best man, slurring his vows. It was a pitiful sight, to say the least. The night of the wedding, I had to literally drag him out of the house into the car and take him to the ER. They pumped his stomach and put him on intravenous fluids to flush his system. The doctor asked me to step out in the hallway and told me of his history and encouraged me to walk away because he was not going to get better. Did I listen? NO! It seems so absurd, in retrospect. Our honeymoon was spent in the ER that night. He was released later the next day. We did not talk at all in the car on the way home. I was so ashamed of Tim and myself for being in this predicament that I could not tell his parents what had happened. I simply could not find the words to say. The following Monday, I received a call from the Pastor telling me our marriage license had expired so the wedding was not official. WHAT?! That should have been my way out, but no…Miss Co-Dependent here told Tim the license expired, which meant we were not actually married. He professed his love to me, again, and I fell for it, hook, line, and sinker! I should have just left right then on the spot, but he convinced me to go to the courthouse and make it official. A couple of months, later things started taking a turn for the worse…as if things were not already bad enough. Tim did not come home one night and would not answer any of my calls. I received a message from my daughter-in-law asking me if I had seen Tim's Facebook post that morning. She told me to get on Facebook to see for myself. To my surprise, and for the whole world to see, it said, "Engaged to my sweet Southern Belle." I knew he was not talking about me; we were already married. I made arrangements for my friends to be on standby the next time he left to come to help me get all my stuff out of the house. I also reconnected with my friend, Gary, who had recently been released from prison, to see if I could move in with him temporarily.

When Tim came back home the next day, I confronted him. He told me he hated me and wanted to be with someone who understood him, which translated into he wanted someone to do drugs with. *"You should leave now. Do not leave a single hair behind because if I find it, I will put a curse on you."* The look on his face shook me, and he knew it. He left the house, and I called my friends. In a matter of moments, nine people were at the house helping me get my stuff out of the house and moved into Gary's apartment. He and I picked up where we left off, as crazy as it sounds. I felt I owed it to him since he was letting me stay there, rent-free.

The divorce drug out for several months, despite Tim, telling me he wanted the divorce. He repeatedly postponed the hearings and made lame excuses as to why he could not make it. He and his fiancé, the "sweet Southern Belle," moved a couple of times while the divorce was pending. Finally, I got my day in court, and the judge granted the divorce.

What I learned from this divorce:

- If you have a check, in your spirit, or a reservation about marrying someone or even dating someone, LISTEN TO IT.
- If friends, family members, or professionals tell you to steer clear from someone or a situation, do not dismiss them. Often, they can see things you cannot.
- You should not ever allow yourself to be guilted into doing anything. If you are not entering into a relationship for the right reasons, it will not work.
- Do not make excuses for others.
- When someone shows you who they are, believe them.

An Unfortunate Fate

Gary and I continued a relationship for another nine months before his addiction got the best of him. I truly loved him and hoped I could help him get past it. Unfortunately, addiction won. He started huffing cans of aerosol and started binging on Coricidin HBP pills. He became suicidal on several occasions and had to be institutionalized. I begged the State to intervene by placing him in a long-term treatment facility. They said they could not do that since he had no insurance; they were not willing to foot the bill. He was released into my care, despite my reservations, and within hours he was drunk and high and ended up bashing my face in, giving me a concussion, and breaking my nose in front of my 18-month-old granddaughter. Gary went to jail, and I moved from Indiana to Kentucky to get away.

What I learned from this mess:

A geographical change does not change anything.
I may have moved locations, but the lies I had believed about myself followed me. I ended up becoming addicted to porn and having several sexual encounters with different men, which left me feeling even worse. I was good enough until they got what they wanted, and they would all just walk away. Each time I gave myself away, I gave a part of my soul to them.

A couple of years later, Gary found out where I was working and started calling me to threaten my life for ruining his. He told me he was not finished with me, and our relationship would not be over until *he* said it was over. He went on to tell me one day when I least expect it; he would come out of the darkness. He spoke of how he wanted to abduct me, brutally rape me, kill me, and then kill himself. He was a tormented soul; I took his threats seriously. After all, his addiction had taken him to depths I never thought he would go and made him do things I never thought he would be capable of. I lived in fear, wondering when I would run into him.

Thankfully, he never made it to Kentucky, but it was not because he had come to his senses or finally given up his rage towards me. No, he never made it to Kentucky for an entirely different reason. On March 28th, 2015, my son called me to tell me he saw in the local newspaper that Gary was found dead in a hotel room from an overdose and laid there three days before anyone found him. I believe they found 20+ empty cans of aerosol around him. I cried many tears over his passing, some were tears of relief, and others were of outright sadness at a senseless loss of life.

I have been through one failed relationship after another. In this chapter, I have covered four of my five divorces, and one of MANY failed relationships. My last divorce would be a book by

itself. You have read my story. Let me ask you, *"Who is to blame?"* Do I suffice it to say all men are out to get what they can get? I assure you I could point my finger and blame all the men I have been with for the mess my life came to be, but that would not serve me well at all. We all go through painful things, and we all have a choice to make…either we will become bitter or better. What will you choose? If you choose to harbor unforgiveness, you will become bitter; if you choose to forgive, you will become better. Please understand I am not saying you must agree with what has been done to you. Likewise, I am not saying that you deserve what happened to you. What I am saying is life is way too short to hold on to offenses and pain you have endured.

Forgiveness is not for the offender; it is for YOU.

Who do you need to forgive?

_____

_____

_____

_____

_____

_____

God has helped me learn from all these experiences. Truthfully, had I not gone through all the crap I have, I would not have an appreciation for the redemptive work of the cross. In the past year,

God has helped me forgive each and every person who has ever wronged me. Surprisingly, the person I had the hardest time forgiving was MYSELF. Why did I need to forgive myself? I am glad you asked! I had to forgive myself for agreeing with all the lies that have been spoken over me, for believing so little of myself, and so little of what Jesus did for me on the cross.

Sadly, I have spent my entire life looking for love. Perhaps, you can relate? God put that desire in your heart because He wants you to find it in Him.

He, alone, can fill every longing of your heart. Believing the lies of the enemy robbed me of my dignity and peace and kept me from knowing my true worth. Your worth and identity do not come from what others say about you, what you have done, or where you are from. Something's worth is determined by the price another is willing to pay for it.

Dear one, Jesus paid the ultimate cost when He died for you. That makes you priceless!

Today, I know who I am; I am no longer bound to my past. It is my prayer that my story has somehow caused you to pinpoint when and where the embers were placed in *your* life, so the enemy is exposed. More importantly, I want to glorify God, the power of the cross, and share the unconditional, perfect love of God. Give Him the charred remains of your life, and He will give you beauty for ashes!

Shawna Dillon

madebyapple75@gmail.com

Shawna Dillon has experienced multiple separations and reconciliations for over nine years before she divorced from her first husband. Shawna, has one brother, who is her twin. She has a master's degree in Organizational Management with a specialization in Healthcare Organization.

Shawna's and her current husband have been married for just over eight years. She is a member of the First Christian Church (Disciples of Christ), where she serves as a Deacon and member of the board.

Shawna has two Dachshunds that are sisters, one is blind and deaf, but they are the sweetest. Shawna currently works from home as a funding specialist for a durable medical equipment company. She also works as a Pampered Chef consultant, and in her spare time, she loves crafting projects.

Favorite Scripture

Psalm 23 (KJV)

The LORD is my shepherd; I shall not want.
He maketh me to lie down in green pastures: he leadeth me beside the still waters.
He restoreth my soul: he leadeth me in the paths of righteousness for his name's sake.
Yea, though I walk through the valley of the shadow of death, I will fear no evil: for thou art with me; thy rod and thy staff they comfort me. Thou preparest a table before me in the presence of mine enemies: thou anointest my head with oil; my cup runneth over. Surely goodness and mercy shall follow me all the days of my life: and I will dwell in the house of the LORD forever.

Dedication

I would like to dedicate this chapter to my mom. My mom has been my rock ever since I was born, raising two kids on her own. Through every up and down in my life, she has always been standing at my side.

I am Strong Enough

By: Shawna Dillion

When I was young, I always dreamed of having that fairy tale wedding like you see on television. My colors were going to be pink and white, and my dress would make me look like a princess. I had those dreams throughout my entire childhood. When I was growing up, I had many friends but never really dated much, even through high school. I played the flute in band, was on the academic team, and in other groups until I graduated in 1993. Moving out to go to college was a huge change because it was the first time being on my own. I was very thankful that I was only an hour away from home and had many friends that would be attending with me.

Fall of 1993 was my first semester in college at Morehead State University, and academically not what it should have been. I planned on being a physical therapist when I started, and after my first semester, I had no idea what I wanted to major in. After failing many of my classes, I was hoping my spring semester might be better. However, I was enjoying hanging out more than studying, and my grades continued to suffer. Since I needed to make up some classes and get my head in the game, I attended both summer sessions in 1994. There were not many people on campus, and most of my friends were gone, so I was able to get myself back on track.

Second Year of College

In the fall semester of 1994, I met a man that I instantly became good friends with. He was not like any guy that I had been around before, and something just drew me closer and closer to him, and I wanted to hang out with him all the time. I continued to stay focused more than I had the year before. I spent a lot of late nights with friends, going back to the dorm to study. In December I was at a party. People were going back and forth from one apartment to another, hanging out. I was feeling sick and just sitting around no knowing this party would be a huge turning point in my life because I was physically assaulted by someone that I did not know. I was embarrassed and blamed myself and left immediately after and did not tell anyone what had happened. The following day the few people I told, including the guy I had a crush on, talked me into going to the hospital to get checked out. I finished the semester and received some counseling on campus regarding the incident.

At the end of the semester, I decided to move back home and go to a local community college during the spring of 1995. I needed some time to myself and time to focus on my studies. I finally was able to get my grades up and think about what I wanted to do with my life. Even though I had moved back home, I was still seeing the man who became my future husband. He would drive in over the weekends and pick me up. We would hang out with some of my friends or go out to eat just to spend time together. Every time he said goodbye, I missed him so much. I was never sure how to react to my feelings for him.

I Said Yes!

When the spring semester ended, he kept asking me to come to Morehead for a visit. The week prior to me going to Morehead, there was a tornado that came through and did some damage close to where he was living. So, over Memorial Day weekend in 1995, I went to Morehead to hang out with friends and, of course, check on my boyfriend. My mother had asked me if I was going to see him and I said yes but others as well. The following day when it was time for me to drive home, my boyfriend gave me two options. I could drive home and be unsure when we would see each other again, or we could get married. At first, I just laughed, and he explained how serious he was and how he thought that we were meant to be together. So, after laughing and talking for a few hours, I said yes.

Here I am getting married, I should have called home, but I knew it was a Friday and my mom would be at work. We went to Walmart and got cheap wedding bands, then to the courthouse. For the first time, I realized I would not have my fairy tale wedding. I stood my ground, declaring I would not get married in the courthouse; it had to be in church. We spent a couple of hours calling the local churches to see if anyone would marry us on such short notice, and we finally found someone. I will never forget the day because all my dreams vanished. I did not even get married in a dress; I only had shorts and a dress shirt with me. When we arrived at the church, the preacher did show his concern and stated if I were his daughter, he would be upset. Nevertheless, he agreed to marry us. There were two older ladies in the church that agreed to be witnesses. We were asked if we wanted the long or short version, and we both agreed to short, all though it seemed like he talked forever, and at one point, I thought my husband was going to pass out from being so nervous.

Time to Tell the Family

After the so-called wedding, we got in our separate cars to drive back home. I had to return my mom's car that I had borrowed and tell everyone the news. The entire hour drive, I was crying. I was happy and sad. How was I going to tell my mom that I had just gone off and gotten married? I was about to break her heart. Sure enough, when she got home, we were sitting in the den and my grandmother, the "tell it like it is" person, just blurted out, "guess who got married"? My mother went straight to her room; I knew she was devastated. She finally came out of her room and did not have much to say. I packed a small bag because next, we had to go and tell his parents. Thankfully, they only lived about 30 minutes away. They were just as shocked as my mom was, considering I had never even met them. Over the next couple of days, all my family was in town for our family reunion, and the remainder of them found out that I had run off and gotten married. Some were very happy for me and told me how I had a glow about me, and some, I know, just kept their comments to themselves.

Where are We Going to Live?

After the long holiday weekend was over and staying with family, I finally realized I had no clue as to where we were going to live. My husband had to go to work on Tuesday. He was renting a place in Morehead with two roommates, who where they were not happy with the arrangement of me staying there with them for the time being. His lease was going to be up in two months, so that gave us a little time to figure things out. During this time my husband got the idea to move to Charlotte, North Carolina. He had lived there before and always enjoyed it. I had only been to North Carolina on high school trips. We agreed on North Carolina and just started driving, my family had no idea where I was until I called them. This was the first time I had ever had a Krispy Kreme doughnut, and I have been in love ever since. I was so lonely; I missed my family terribly. So, after being there for three weeks, we drove back home, and he gave up the job search. In the next couple of weeks, we split our time between our family's homes. While there, my mom began planning and hosting a bridal shower. She did not get to give me a wedding, so this was her way of making up for it. My life was not starting out the way I always dreamt; none the less I was happy.

Third Year of College

Now that all the traveling was over, I had to decide about school. I decided to enroll back in at Morehead for the 1995 fall semester because my husband had finally found another job as a manager at a local pizza store there. Since I was going to school, we were approved to live in married housing. This had to be the smallest apartment ever. There was a small room with a kitchen area, a hall that had a closet and was considered a bedroom, and a small bathroom. Nonetheless, it was on campus. After a couple of months, I started to have doubts for the first time, then again, I was in love. We had very little money and just scraped by. Good thing rent was cheap, and utilities were included. To help make my husband's numbers look good at work, late at night, he would send the workers home and come get me to help out in the store. Even though I did not get paid, I worked hard cleaning the store and helping prep for the next day. Sometimes during the day, he would have a driver bring me lunch. Pizza and breadsticks seem to be meals most of the time for both of us, all though it could have been a lot worse. This did not help my self-image as I was never skinny and eating the way we were was not helping. I was at least getting exercise as I did not have a car and had to walk to all my classes.

My Husband was an Alcoholic

I knew when I met my husband that he liked to drink, and I was okay with that. For some reason, I thought that since we were married, the drinking would slow down. Boy, was I wrong. Any extra money that we seem to have was all spent on alcohol and cigarettes. I never had any issues with someone drinking or smoking, but when it is a habit that you can never get enough of and you see it changing people, it makes a difference. It started getting to a point that I could see major changes. At first, when we were getting ready to go out, he started making comments about my hair and why I was not wearing makeup. I was never really the person that wore makeup, and he would always say you are so pretty with makeup on why do you not wear it more often. I wanted to be a good wife and started wearing it more even though I hated it. I started struggling with my classes again because I did not have enough time to study and do my homework. When he got home from work, he wanted to go out to party, and this meant that I was the designated driver. We lived in Morehead, and there were not many places to go out and party in town, so most times it was driving an hour or more away. The worst thing I learned quickly was that when my husband got drunk, he wanted to fight the world because he was not a happy drunk. I could not handle all this time out on the town, and some time since I was under twenty-one, I would be sitting in the car in the parking lot waiting for him to come out. I finally stopped going and told him if he wanted to go out, then he was going to have to find someone to drive him because I could not continue down this path.

I Left my Husband

At the end of the spring semester in 1996, I decided to take the summer off from classes and decided to leave my husband. At this point, he was drinking non-stop and had been fired from his job for not showing up to work. We completely broke ties. I did not know where he moved to, or where he was working since, he got fired in Morehead and changed his phone number. I filed for divorce, but since we could not find him, we could not serve him with the papers. This went on for months, and I decided to stay home and go back to the local community college for the 1996 fall semester. Life seemed to be getting better, and so were my grades. I was riding with one of my girlfriends back and forth that was also going to school there since I did not have a car. My mom wanted me to focus on my schooling, so she helped pay some of my bills and chip in for gas, so I did not have to get a job.

New Year's Eve 1997, I decided to go out to a party with friends, and that is when I panicked. I found my ex-husband at the last place I thought he would be. We had decided to order pizza, and I always got talked into ordering the food, so I placed the call, and he answered the phone at a pizza store the next town over. I quickly hung up, and my friends wanted to know what was wrong. It was a voice that I would never forget. He did not even have to say his name. He said hello twice, and I could not speak. Someone else called and ordered the pizza, and after the holidays were over, I contacted my attorney's office and was finally able to get the divorce papers served to him. What a relief! I was starting to think it was about to be over, but I was completely wrong.

My Husband Came Around

During the spring semester in 1997, one day after class, I was walking out to my mom's car and found my husband standing there. I first started to turn around and walk away, but I needed to know why he had not signed the divorce papers yet. He said he wanted to talk, so; I followed him over to a nearby restaurant because I wanted to be in public and honestly did not really feel too comfortable in the middle of a parking lot. After talking for what seemed like hours hearing, how sorry he was, and how over the last several months he had stopped drinking and wanted to try to save our marriage, I told him I was not going to rush back into something I had spent months trying to get out of. At this point, I decided to keep my speaking to him a secret from everyone, even my friends. I kept going to classes, and we started going on dates again.

Around Easter, I had made the decision to get baptized in the church I had grown up in. I felt strongly about it and knew I was ready to live my life in Christ. My mind kept wondering about my marriage, how I should not walk away, and how I should try to make it work. He was living with friends that I knew he partied with them in the past, and I told him that as long as he lived with them, he would never be sober, and he had to make a choice. We kept everything a secret until he was able to find a job, and we made the decision to reunite.

The First Time I Took My Husband Back

During the summer of 1997, I had reapplied to Morehead and was accepted back in. I was focused on my schoolwork and wanted to succeed in life. This should have been my fourth year and a senior, but I was barely a junior due to bad grades and changing schools.

I had also made the decision against my family's wishes to give my husband another chance. I moved back to Morehead, and my husband and I had found a trailer to rent just outside of town. For months things for the first time seemed to be really good between us. I was going to school, and my husband was working. We discussed starting a family, found out that my health issues may be a problem, and I was having a difficult time. This took a toll on both of us, and soon my husband slowly but surely started having a drink here and there. The holidays were getting close, and he had already driven to his parents while I finished my classes before Thanksgiving. While I was home alone washing dishes, a glass shattered, and I almost lost one of my fingers on my right hand. I was able to get a towel and walk to a friend's who was living in the same trailer court. However, they were all drinking, and I had to drive myself to the hospital.

When I got to the ER, I was there for what seemed like forever until they could get the bleeding to stop. I had to have several stitches inside and out on my hand and taking the exam the next day was extremely hard. However, I did get out of washing dishes for several weeks, and to this day, I will not stick my hand down in a glass to wash it. I drove home to my mom's house and spent time with my family over a long Thanksgiving weekend. I called my husband, and he stated he was hanging out with friends and family, so I went back to Morehead since I had a class on Monday. We hardly spoke for several days. My gut was telling me something was wrong. He was not answering his phone or returning my calls.

The Alcoholic Returned

After he had been gone for several days, I returned home from class, and he was there. He had nothing to say except that he was

catching up with friends, and yes, there was drinking and parties, but nothing major. The pattern was starting over, more alcohol in the house, and he was going out and staying gone all night. The worst part of his getting drunk was that he did not want to get up the next day, so the cycle of missing work again or calling in sick was repeating itself. We only lived on one salary and whatever I had left over from grants and student loans.

One night after class, I came home, and there were several people there, some I knew, and some I had never seen before. Friends of his from home had come down on a Thursday night to go out partying with my husband. I stood up to my husband, who was already drinking and said I do not want them here, and I do not want you going out with them. This, of course, started a big argument in which he drew back and hit me. When I ducked, he hit my arm. Now I have been able to defend myself, so once he hit me, I threw a couple of punches back at him. Once his friends heard us arguing, and he left the bedroom, I heard them say we must leave before she calls the cops, and they did. I sat there all night, hardly closing my eyes because I knew that this was the beginning of the end. This time he was gone for a week with no contact. I knew that I had taken a lot of verbal abuse over the past couple of years. However, he had never really gotten to the point of getting so mad at me to hit me. I kept quiet for weeks and just let him do his thing. I finally told my mom that I was leaving him at the end of the spring semester and moving back home.

Leaving for the Second Time

We made it another year. At the end of the spring semester of 1998, it was time to rent yet another U-Haul and move my stuff back home. I packed everything that was mine and moved out without telling my husband since he was gone on yet another drinking binge. I figured if he is going to go on week-long drinking binges, I could leave whenever I wanted. Classes were over for the summer, and back home I went. The summer was good. I hung out with friends and family and got some much-needed rest. I needed to decide if I wanted to stay registered at Morehead or back to the community college. I decided for the fall of 1998 semester to go back to the local community college.

During the fall semester, I started talking to a gentleman in my class who was going through a divorce like I was. It felt good talking to him because he was going through the same things I was. It was more of friendship and nothing serious. I did not feel like I could talk about my issues to most of my friends or family because they did not know what I was going through. There were only one or two people that knew how bad my marriage had gotten. Surprisingly, things were going well through the fall and into the spring semester.

My Husband Opened a Business

My husband started reaching out in the spring of 1999, and we did talk a few times. He seemed to have changed some. He had moved back home and started a carpet cleaning business for himself. This was something he had always been interested in since he had left Charlotte North Carolina years ago. He had been in a bad car wreck with family while we were separated, received a settlement, and invested it into opening the business. His sister worked for him for little to no money but seemed to be doing well. His company was the only one in the area at the time that dyed carpet. He had rented a small office to keep some equipment in and had a phone line setup. It seemed from the outside to be a busy and productive business. He showed me where he was living, and I did go see him a couple of times. I told him that I could not get involved with him anymore and that we were better being friends than we were at being married and that we really should get divorced. During this time, I was helping family members that were sick and needed twenty-four-hour care. During the week, I would go and spend the night at their house to help take care of them. This prevented me from making the full commitment to get back with him. There was too much going on in my personal and family life.

Falsely Accused

In the summer of 1999, one night around three or four am, someone was ringing the doorbell and woke my mother and me up. I was afraid it was my husband. It was not. It was the police, and they were there to serve me with a subpoena to appear in court because I had allegedly damaged my husband's company van and set it on fire. There was also a restraining order attached. I cried for hours and hours; my mother never said a word. I had no idea what had happened or what was going on. All I knew was that whatever happened, I was getting blamed for it.

My family members were in worse shape health-wise, causing me to attend my first court appearance alone. I really could not afford an attorney and knew I had done nothing wrong. If I were going to need an attorney, I would have the court appoint one for me. I sat in the courtroom for hours, and my case was finally called. I was the only one that showed up. My husband and his friends, who were witnesses, never showed up, and they moved my case to another day. In the following days, one of my family members passed away, and it was a difficult couple of weeks, because I knew I would have to go back to court. The second court appearance came up, and the same thing happened again. Only I showed up, and the charges and restraining order were dropped.

The Second Time I Took my Husband Back

The following month my husband contacted me again, and the first thing I told him was to stay away, or this time I would be getting the restraining order. He understood and wanted to talk, so we did I wanted to talk about getting the divorce, and he told me that his friends actually destroyed his van while drinking and blamed me for it. To impress his friends, he put me through all of this. He also told me that his friends were sitting in the back of the courtroom to tell him what went on as he never wanted to charge me with anything. I did not know what to think. I was an emotional wreck. Between helping with family members that were sick and taking care of them, going to court, and trying to go to school, the summer of 1999 is a time, I would much rather forget.

Since this was really the only man that I had ever loved, my feelings got the best of me, and we started dating again. He was in a camping mood for the first time since I had known him. I am not the lay on the ground in a tent type of girl. For one, the bugs eat me up and two, I do not like being out in the woods. Thirdly, and the worst, he would let his sister and her boyfriend have a few drinks, and this made me feel so uncomfortable that I would not go places with them. He finally agreed that he was not a good influence on his sister, who, out of the blue, got married to her boyfriend.

When looking for a place to live, we moved into a house close to my family since we were still dealing with illness. I continued to go to the community college for the fall semester of 1999. I got my first job at the local Wendy's restaurant. My husband was not working much. He was cleaning carpets occasionally. I would go to classes during the day and work at night to make just enough for us to survive.

A couple of months later, another family member passed away, which left many of us heartbroken. It would not be long before my husband would go on the drinking binges again. I kept on working while he stayed home and did nothing. We could barely afford rent. My mom would take me to work and come and pick me up at the end of my shift most nights because my husband was too drunk to drive. This time his family did a little intervention, and he sobered up for a few weeks. We moved so I would not have to drive as far to classes and still be close to family. He was working on and off with the carpet cleaning business, we celebrated the holidays, and things seemed to be going well. Then another family tragedy struck.

I Left a Third Time

My husband had a family member that lost a child, and this was hard on everyone, especially me. I had been trying and unable to get pregnant. I would never wish the loss of a child on anyone. A couple of months later, my husband said that he wanted to expand his business and wanted to try to get in the central Kentucky market, and I agreed.

Soon after, he rented an apartment in Winchester, and I continued to stay in Prestonsburg to continue school in the trailer that we were renting. The time apart was getting longer and longer. There was always an excuse for him not coming home or for me not to go there over the weekend. I found out that he had been hosting parties with his friends, and they were staying there with him most of the time. I woke up one morning when the landlord was putting an eviction letter on our door for not paying our rent. While I started packing, I attempted to call my husband over several days, but to no avail. Once again, I made the lonely call to my mom, saying I needed to move home, and as always, her arms and home were open to me no matter what was going on.

I Started Counseling

Now I have left my husband a third time, and I honestly had lost all hope of ever being happy. I needed to continue with school because I needed to finish and prove I could make something of myself. I continued the spring 2000 semester at the local community college. I had started seeing a counselor in Lexington. My grandmother would make the trip with me, so I was not driving alone. I became a nervous wreck because I let everything over the past several years consume me. I never really dealt with the physical assault and the verbal abuse from my husband. I was going twice a week on days when I did not have classes. This was when I really learned about how much verbal abuse I had taken. After I completed counseling, I wanted to make sure that I would be able to help others in some way, so I decided I would start taking more sociology classes to figure out my path in life.

Moving back to Morehead

I had made the decision for the fall of 2000 that I was ready to go back to Morehead and finish my education. My mom and I made a trip to Morehead to look for an apartment; I did not need much it was just my dog and me. We found a small apartment; however, they did not want pets, so I gave my dog to my brother to watch while I was renting. My brother had my dog for about two weeks, and I could not live without him anymore, so I brought him back with me and kept him. My mom had paid the semester's rent, and for a parking spot in the middle of campus, so I did not have to walk over a mile to class. I was on my feet again and doing well. I

was finally happy with myself and living on my own. I had some classes that I had fallen in love with. I remember my favorites were women's health and, of course, a sociology class. I started making friends, was finally enjoying study groups, and coming out of my shy self.

I Wanted a Divorce

Freedom was something that I had not felt in years. I always had those doubts that I was never good enough for my husband or anyone else. It was time to move on and force a divorce on my husband somehow, even if he refused to sign the papers. I was back in touch with an attorney that I had worked with the first time I attempted to get a divorce. We started by sending paperwork to his parents' house since I had no idea where he was living or any way to contact him. Weeks went by, and I received a letter at my mom's house. I read the letter and found out that he had been in jail for a couple of weeks for writing cold checks. He was now in a hospital where he was being treated for bipolar disorder, which after thinking and reading about it, made a lot of sense to me. I decided to go and see him while he was in the hospital because even though I wanted to be done with him, my heart knew that if I could help him, I should. I went to a couple of group sessions and some counseling sessions while he was there. We sorted out a lot of issues, why we had separated three times, and deep down still loved each other. He also realized that he was an alcoholic and that all it took was one drink and he would be on the wagon again.

Third Time I Took my Husband Back

What is wrong with me? How could I still love someone who had treated me so badly over the last couple of years? This man always told me I would never find anyone else, that I was not the best cook, and found faults in everything that I did. I prayed and prayed, and not wanting my marriage to fail decided to give him another chance. He moved in, and he found a job about 45 minutes away. I continued with my classwork but knew I had to take a break and find someplace closer to where he worked for us to pay our bills. At the end of the fall 2000 semester and before we moved, we found another dog, so now we had a boy named Dobbie and a girl named Ivy.

We Moved to a New Town

We moved in December 2000 to the outskirts of Richmond where we found a house, we put a contract on. We were getting ready for the holidays. Life was good, he had a good-paying job, and since I was not working, I spent most of my days watching my nephew. A couple of months later, I found a job at a service station, and between the two of us, we were doing great for the first time ever. We could pay all our bills and had a few dollars in our pockets. The family would come and see us, and we loved the area we were in and the house. In spring 2001, my mother helped put in a pool and loved the summer relaxing in it. We were making our house a home, and everything seemed right in the world. With inheritance that I had received from family, I purchased my very first car; things could not get any better.

I Wanted a Family

Since things were going so well, we decided it was time to try and start a family again. I have had health issues my entire life, so I went to the doctor to see what we could do. I went through all kinds of testing to try and find out the main problem. My doctor told us that it was going to be hard to have a family, and I started taking some medication to try and help. We made good money but not enough to pay for full treatments. This became an incredibly stressful couple of months, having to keep a calendar, take one pill on this day, another pill on these days, and every time I took a pregnancy test, it was negative. My heart sank more and more. During this time, my hormones were crazy, and within four to five months, I had gained almost eighty pounds. My husband and I made the decision to stop all the medication. I came to realize that my body was just not going to let me have children. I went into a very dark depression, kept gaining weight, and blindly going day by day. I could not understand why it was so hard. I wanted to have a child so bad but settled with my two dogs. My faith was suffering, I did not know how to make things right, and it felt like I had slipped completely away from my faith and God.

My Grandmother was Sick

I was already in a dark place. My husband and I were both dealing with our emotions. My grandmother started having health issues, and after some testing, she was diagnosed with lung cancer. Cancer has been very well known in my family and especially on my grandmother's side. My nephew was just two years old and my grandmother loved him more than anything. She decided that she wanted to live as long as she could to watch him grow up so she decided to have lung surgery, and have a lung removed. Where I currently worked, they would not let me take a week off to attend her surgery, so I decided to quit because I needed to be with my family. The week before her surgery, she wanted to have family photos taken with everyone just in case something happened. This was a family event, and many photos were taken. My husband and I took our first real set of photos.

It was time to head to the hospital, and my grandmother had made comments that she did not think she would ever be back home. The surgery went well, and everything seemed to be good. She was doing well. A few days later, they came in and told her that she would have to take treatments because the cancer has spread to her lymph nodes and progressed more than they had thought. That night I believe she gave up the fight, and she had a massive heart attack. My mother and I rushed to the hospital and was able to see her during the 6 am visitation in ICU. After that, we never got to see her again. I know they did all they could, but a big part of my life was gone. I am not sure if she had spoken to God. She believed she would never come home, and she was right.

Around a week later, all the family photos came in. This brought up a lot of emotions seeing her again for the last time. This was a hard time for our family and especially for my mother even to this day. After my grandmother's passing, my family was never really the same. We have not been together much for Christmas because my mother lives in Florida full time, and we are unable to all get together. We came from an extremely large family, and it has now dwindled to my mother, brother, nephew, and myself.

Seeking Employment

I had taken some time off to grieve, and after the New Year, I needed to find another job as soon as I could. It was hard living on just my husband's income. He was supportive of me taking the time I needed to grieve. However, I needed out of the house. In January 2002, I was hired at another local service station as a cashier. Soon after, the store manager was promoted to regional manager I took the position of the store manager. I was making really good money, and my numbers and inventory were looking great. After working there for a year, I started to struggle.

I was working seven days a week for a couple of months and asked my manager for a weekend off for rest and spend time with my mother before she went back to Florida. I was unsure when I would see her again. My manager told me that I could not have the weekend off, so I turned in my keys and walked out. I had enough, and my body was so tired. It was a battle. I was first denied my unemployment, so I appealed, and once they found out how long I had worked without a day off, they overturned my denial. This only helped with my back pay. We could not live on my unemployment and my husband's salary alone. I found another job in another service station this time working as a cook. The station was just at the entrance of an industrial park, so it was busy from breakfast until the counter shut down. This was harder than working in a restaurant. I was having to wedge about fifty pounds of potatoes a day, make pizza, help with hotdogs, and burgers.

Working with My Husband

My husband told me they were hiring, where he worked in the local call center, where I had always said I did not want to work, but the cooking job was killing me, so I finally applied in 2003. I was hired as a contractor, and the account I was working with decided they did not want contractors working for them, so my team was quickly hired as a permanent employee. This did not sit well with my husband because it took him over two years to get hired.

My mother was up for the fall, and she purchased a new puppy. When I saw her for the first time, I was in love. One of my dogs could not have babies and was having false pregnancies. The vet had recommended we get her a baby. So now we had three dogs and loved them all. One day I started feeling bad and having severe chest pains. I had been on blood pressure medicine since I was around seventeen, and when I contacted my heart doctor, they said to go to the emergency room. My husband was so nervous I ended up driving us over to the hospital. After getting checked out, thankfully, I did not have a stroke or heart attack. However, I did have some infection in my heart cavity. This got me thinking and worried about everyone around me and some of my life choices. I needed to take better care of myself.

My Husband Left Me

My husband's grandmother had taken ill and was in a local hospital in the fall of 2003. A few days later, she passed. Things were about to take a turn for the worse. His grandmother had done so much for him, treated him like her own child, and it was a trying time for him. After the funeral, alcohol started making an appearance in the house; one beer can at a time. I was up late at night crying, wondering where he was and when he was coming home. I was alone again for the first time in around three years, compared to this being the longest and happiest time that my husband and I shared. He started hanging out with younger guys from work, and when they would get off their night shift, he would tell me someone was driving him home, and I did not need to pick him up.

It was my birthday, and we were driving home from work, which was around a forty-five-minute drive. He had not even told me happy birthday that day, and when we got home, he told me that he was leaving. We argued and fought for what seems like hours while he packed a suitcase, all he would say was he was not happy, wanted to leave, and one of his friends was coming to pick him up. He had been on a low carb diet for about two or three months and had lost about seventy pounds, so I asked him if he was seeing someone else, and he denied it. I had to continue to go to work and

see him in the building, and the word was already around that he had moved out. The worst part is that they were talking about how bad of a person I was and that he had put up with me for as long as he could. I guess he thought I would quit, but if I were going to be on my own, I needed the job and the benefits. I could not afford to leave.

I Needed a Place to Live

A few days later, I decided to change the locks on the doors because I knew he was not coming back, and I did not want any of my stuff to disappear while I was at work. This made him extremely angry. This also ensured he had to see me when he came to get clothes. At this point, all his clothes had been thrown on the floor in a bedroom. He soon stopped coming by.

I knew on my salary, I could not afford to stay in the house that we had made a home, and in December 2003, I had started looking for an apartment. I also needed to get my money moved to another bank, so he did not have access to it. I set up my own bank account and quickly had my direct deposit moved from work so he could not take it. I then set up a P.O. box because I did not want him to know where I had moved to and forwarded all my mail to the post office. I finally found an apartment that would let me keep my dogs, so immediately after Christmas, I packed all that I could and moved from a three-bedroom house into a two-bedroom townhouse and rented out a storage building.

My Husband got Engaged

We continued to work in the same building. I kept asking from day one if he was seeing someone else, and he always denied it. However, the truth eventually emerged. He had moved in with his supervisor that had moved down from Michigan the same day he moved out from me. I could not afford to file for divorce on my low income and told him that since he left me, he needed to pay for the divorce.

In the early spring of 2004, I had to have surgery to remove my tonsils. I had been sick for months, after trying several medications, my tonsils would never go back down, so they had to come out. After returning to work, things kept moving along, and I was doing well at work. My husband had switched shifts so that we were not in the building at the same time. This made me feel better. Come June, my husband finally paid an attorney to file for a divorce. He had finally agreed because he had proposed to his girlfriend and they had already set a wedding date in July. A few people were asking me what I had thought about it. I just said, well, I am happy for him, but he may want to get divorced before their wedding date. Once it got out around work that he was not divorced yet, then some of my co-workers that had been listening to what he said about our split began to wonder what really happened.

Divorce was Final

We had already lost everything we had together, so I agreed to the paperwork and I signed the divorce. It would be final in 30 days. In July 2004 it was finally real, the long journey that started in May 1995 was going to be over in a few days. My ex remarried around twenty days from the date our divorce was final. Even though the last eight to nine years contained some of the hardest moments in my life, the hard part was just beginning. Who am I now? I married when I was nineteen and did not know really who I was or who I wanted to be.

After the divorce was final, that is when I honestly knew we would never be together again. I had gone through the motions so many times before, and he always came back. Now, he was never coming back, and I was completely alone. Every night was a hard night. There were so many tears I could have filled a bathtub. I felt so sorry rethinking all the negative things he said to me; you will never be good enough, no one else will ever want you, and much more. Those words from the past and our previous separations haunted me day and night. Finally, I received a little bit of good news. He was leaving Kentucky and moving back to Michigan with his supervisor/wife. I felt like a small weight was lifted. I was no longer wondering if I would run into him at the store or work. It was a small miracle.

Being Alone

For the first few months, I went to work, only did what I had to do, and then back to my apartment. Work was going well, I was promoted to a team leader, and then about a year later to a supervisor. I loved my job and the company that I worked for. If my dogs could talk, they could have written my story for me, because they were my companions and the only ones that knew what I was dealing with. I finally started hanging out with some friends at work and allowed alcohol to start creeping into my life. It started by hanging out and having a drink here and there. Soon it ended up being something that helped me sleep at night.

I finally found a mixture of friends that became more than friends. They were like brothers and sisters to me. We talked about life, and I finally had individuals who I could take comfort hanging out with. At this point in my life, I was able to cut out alcohol. Now, I will not say that I have never had a drink since then, but it was no longer a crutch for me. I felt accepted and felt like I was coming out into the world again. We hung out a lot, and at of times, I stayed out way too late and got very few hours of sleep. I managed and was still successful at work. This had become my new norm.

I had found several new friends in my life that helped me through the dark times. Some were younger and some older. But I learned from opening my arms and welcoming all those that accepted me for who I am. To this day, some of these individuals are still my friends. We may not speak every day, although we still have those photos and memories that will forever be in our hearts and minds to become the people that we are today.

My Mother had some Health Issues

My mother would come up during the summers, and over the next couple of years, she had some major surgeries. First, she had knee replacement surgery, and she spent some time at my brother's, who was able to put her a bed downstairs. Then my mother had part of her colon removed due to pre-cancerous spots. Finally, my mother had a hernia repaired from her colon surgery, which seemed to have been the worst. This was my summer for a couple of years, by the time she was ready to head back home, I was ready for my freedom again. I always cherish the time we have together. We also had a couple of sets of puppies and the bad thing about puppies you never want to get rid of them, and it is sad to see them go.

My mother used to tell people inquiring about me that I had multiple boyfriends. Well, this was not true. I hung out with friends, but I knew it was not time for me to date anyone until I found myself and was finally ready to move on from my ex husband. In 2005 while trying to find myself, I realized I needed God back in my life for good and decided to look for a church in the town I lived in. I had not been to church in years. I had been baptized in the church I grew up in. However, that was over an hour away, and I never felt like I was ready to find a new church before. God was ready for me, and the first church I attended opened me with welcome arms. After my first visit, I filled out a visitor card with my contact information, and the preacher called me a few days later. He came and visited me at home, and we talked for some time. He told me that I was welcome and explained that they did not have a large divorce group that attended. I did feel odd at first, but God led me to this church, and that is what I needed in my life. After a year in attendance, I decided to move my membership there. I was active and went to Sunday school, main service, Sunday night service, and Wednesday night. I immersed myself in the church; it had been years, and I had a lot of catching up to do.

My Health Declined

The doctor's visits were becoming more regular. As I mentioned previously, my ex-husband and I tried to have kids but were never able to. After my divorce, I was dealing with more and more pain and started going back to the doctor to help manage the pain. I had issues with my cycle and pain my entire life. To stay balanced, I had been on birth control pills for many years, except when trying to conceive. I came to the final decision that due to the cysts and all the pain having children would never be a possibility. I advised the doctors; I would give them six months to come up with something, then it would be time to remove all my issues surgically.

After I decided to have surgery in the fall of 2006, I met a man, and something between us just clicked. We started hanging out more and more. We got along, and both enjoyed sports. I started hoping this might be someone I could see myself with. I made the decision to be open and honest and let him know that I could never have kids, and in a couple of months would be having surgery. He understood and did not run away like I thought he might. I had a terrible fear that I was not going to be whole anymore, was damaged from divorce, and now I was going to be damaged even more by not being what I would call a full woman. During this time, my uncle passed away, my mom flew back from Florida, and the man I had been seeing was able to watch the dogs for me while I was gone for a few days. He loved the dogs, and everything seemed to be going in a good direction.

Time for Surgery

My surgery was scheduled for March 2007, and it would be life-changing for me. I told my mom there was no reason to come home I could take care of myself. I knew she would freeze in the weather, and in turn, burn me up, and I could not handle that. While I was in the hospital, my boyfriend took care of the dogs at the house. They loved him, but this time they did not eat much when I was away. When I got home, they were so excited they ate so much it was a mess because they had gotten sick.

The first few weeks after surgery was extremely hard, but since I was on salary, I was able to get ten weeks' full pay to recover. During recovery, I discovered that my left leg started going numb if I stood very long, and my lower back would hurt. When I went to the doctor for a checkup, they said that it was not related to surgery. I did an MRI and found out that I had a bulging disk that was pinching a nerve making my leg go numb. Now, I had to adjust how I did things and deal with my leg going numb.

During this time, I attended my first, The Ohio State spring football game with my boyfriend. I had never been to a place that was so big, and it was amazing. Over Memorial Day weekend, my

mom was back up for the summer, and I went with my boyfriend to meet his family for the first time. I call him my boyfriend; however, it was still really unclear what we were at that moment. Part of me was still extremely scared because I was just waiting for something to go wrong and end it all.

Working Together

It was finally time to go back to work. Good thing I sat at a desk the majority of the time. Now my boyfriend was thinking about leaving his job. Even though I had strong doubts, I told him they were hiring in another department where I worked. Was I crazy to attempt to work in the same building with someone I was seeing? The last time ended badly. Was something different this time? He was hired towards the end of summer 2007, and we started riding to work together. This helped me determine if I was with someone who really cared for me. He worked in a different department, but we were on the same shift, so we were together every day. We started talking about moving in together and looking for a place to rent so we would have a shorter commute and save money.

Buying a Home

We found a house instead of an apartment. We were going to look for a place that was for rent and could not find any. We drove by a house that had a for sale sign in the yard. It did not look like anyone lived there. The windows did not have any curtains, and the driveway was empty, so we stopped and peeked into the windows like crazy people. While looking at the back yard, the owner pulled up and asked if we wanted to look inside, and of course, we said yes. The year before, I had worked with a company to see what I could qualify for on my own and had previously looked at a house, but it did not work out. I knew how much house I could afford on my own and my limit if our relationship fell apart. We fell in love with the house and signed a contract. We were going to move in together, and things were finally looking up. A week before my birthday in 2007, we were moved into our house. After getting settled in, we still never put a name on our relationship and left things the way they were because why rock the boat if everything is going well.

I made the decision to go back and finish my degree. I started with online classes while working full time. I enjoyed being back at school. I felt like things were finally falling into place. I finished my BA of Arts in Organizational Management. Work and life were going really well. I had worked many different shifts at work and was able to move to a normal Monday through Friday, 8 am to 5 pm position.

Close to Christmas, I slipped and took a fall in the back yard. When I fell, I heard my foot pop. I broke a bone in my right foot. Good thing I had someone to drive me and worked closely to home. Once I finally got the boot off in a couple of months, it was freedom. However, a few weeks later, in the spring of 2008, I stepped out of the front door, and my leg buckled. I fell again. This time, I broke a bone in my left foot but not as bad, and I only had to wear a boot for a couple of weeks.

Time for God

2010 was going to be a huge year for me. It was time for me to get back into the church. God was missing me, and I was missing Him. Since I was no longer working on Sundays, I had no excuse. There was a church that I could see from my front door. The building is one of those that you really must see to believe. It is over two hundred years old, and the outside is stone, with these beautiful stained-glass windows all around. It was perfect. I drove by for a week or two before I decided to go in. When I arrived, I will never forget the love that a couple showed me in the parking lot. They welcomed me in and even wanted me to sit with them. I felt immediately at home, and I know that God had put me there for a reason. I continued to sit with them and, after a few months, moved my membership to this church, which would become a second home for me.

Time for a Change

During this time, the company I worked for had been bought out by Hewlett-Packard. After taking a pay cut and hearing things, as a supervisor, I knew that when contracts were up for renewal, they were going to be moving them to other centers and eventually close the building in Winchester. My husband was traveling on a special project to Michigan when I decided to interview for something new. Someone I knew had moved to a company in Lexington, which was a call center. Instead of desktop support, this was working with oxygen equipment. I took my chances and was hired as a supervisor to work with inbound calls in the summer of 2010. During training, I learned a lot about oxygen equipment, how to take calls, order supplies when needed, and how to troubleshoot failing equipment. Since I was a supervisor every couple of weeks, I would have to be on-call at home when the center was closed and some of those nights would be sleepless. Unfortunately, I was also stuck working a 10-hour shift, which included Saturdays. The only good thing about working on a Saturday is there were only around six of us in the building, so it was extremely quiet, although a very slow day. I made the decision to go back to school and get my master's degree, so life was crazy and fun all at the same time.

Getting Married

It was time for me to start making wedding plans because I was getting married again in the fall of 2011. I always said after my divorce that I would never marry again. My soon to be husband said he never wanted to get married either. We had lived together for a couple of years and had not hurt or killed each other. It seemed safe enough living together, so we decided it was time. During this time, we went to church for some marriage counseling. A few months before our wedding, my church hired a new preacher. We felt very comfortable with him, and in September, he married us in front of our friends and family. I was finally getting the church wedding that I had wanted my entire life. I worked hard but could not afford a massive wedding. I found a dress shop with the perfect dress that let me make payments; I paid for someone to take pictures, then, of course, paid someone to make our cakes. I did all my decorations with the exception of the flowers; those were a gift from a friend of my mom's in Florida who was a retired florist. I planned and made the food causing the day before to be a mad rush setting up. My future mother in law wanted to know what she could make, and all I wanted was her cheeseball, which has always been a second love in my life. My day was here, and it was perfect, with beautiful weather, one maid of honor and a best man. We did not go anywhere for a honeymoon because we did not want to go into debt for a wedding, and that is not what we needed.

Spiritual Growth

Not only was my life starting anew, so was my church life. I was asked to be on the board at church. I was not sure why, nonetheless I took the chance on growing in the church. I helped with the little kids teaching them on Sunday night or Wednesday night and with other church functions. I continued to grow with the church and would start putting my coupon skills to work when helping with the kitchen and food for event. This was a passion for me and gave me joy. I have grown some lifelong friends and church family. We have laughed and shared tears over the years.

My next two surgeries and getting laid off

Like my spiritual life, work was also going well. I had taken time off for gallbladder surgery in 2012, and now my back was really starting to give me some hard times. It was hard to walk very far, or even sit for very long. I had to walk a lot at work, so it was getting harder and harder to be up on the floor, assisting as much as I should have been. My husband was getting worried, seeing me in so much pain and encouraged me to see a specialist. I went to see a surgeon and decided it was time to have one of the bulging disks in my lower back shaved down to stop it from pinching the nerve in my leg. When I told my manager that I would need at least five weeks off work, they said, well, you better do it sooner rather than later. I thought that was such an odd comment; I would soon know why. The day before I went in for surgery in November 2013, I was off work preparing, but everyone was calling me. Corporate had come in and was having meetings with everyone.

Over one hundred of my co-workers were being laid off. I attempted to find out what was going to happen to me, but all the human resource department would tell me is that they would be in touch. A couple of days after surgery, I finally got the call that I was also being laid off. I was currently on medical leave, so I did not have to go back to work. Those being laid off reported to work for thirty days, and the last thirty would be paid. I did not have to report to work. A couple of weeks later, I went and collected my things.

Seeking New Employment

What were we going to do? I just had back surgery, and the loss of my job made things not look good. I had many at church praying for us, and I started applying for anything that looked like it may be something that I would enjoy. My husband had been at his job for a few years and loved it. Thankfully, his pay was able to hold us over, and he encouraged me to find a job that I would enjoy. I found a job with a durable medical equipment company in Lexington. They asked when I could start, and I said whenever you want me to. I only had one unemployment check, which was not much before I started getting my full paycheck again. I started by working with people that walked in the store and soon found myself working new orders that came across the fax. This was a fast pace environment because we did discharge equipment for oxygen, walkers, wheelchairs, and other medical equipment. I found a love for this type of work. I had a purpose, and I was helping others.

Becoming a Deacon

During this time, I was continuing to grow with the church, and my preacher approached me about becoming a Deacon. My first reaction was to deny his request, not because I was a woman because I thought I was too young. I spoke to my husband and mother regarding this, and they both told me to think and pray about my decision. I did grow up in a church with Deacons and Elders; however, my entire church was made up of an older congregation. Being with younger people in the church was different for me. I decided to become a Deacon and serve.

However, God planned for me to serve well before I made the decision. Life was good again.

I am still, to this day, scared of being a Deacon. I do not have a strong knowledge of the Bible, but I am learning every day. I have stood out of my comfort zone and lead our early morning service during the summer and preached during two regular services. I have never been what you would call rich. We make enough to get by, have a house, food on the table, and we both drive a car. This is rich enough for us.

Job Changes

Soon drama was taking over where I worked, and I was told I would never move up or amount to anything other than a customer service representative. I decided to leave the company. In August 2016, I moved to a company that worked with many hospitals and doctor's offices, releasing medical records. This was a hard decision for my husband and me due to the pay cut. I was a senior representative, and I traveled throughout the state training others and filling in where I was needed. During this time, I put a lot of miles on my car, and some weeks were spent staying in a hotel room. I loved my job; however, I again knew I was not going to be promoted to any higher position and got tired of the driving. When I was hired, I was told it would be no more than an hour away. It was a lot more, and sometimes I would be gone from home for a week at a time. While on vacation in the spring of 2018, I did a phone interview for another durable medical equipment company in Lexington and chose to make the move.

I was back to working with a very close friend, and it was my time to shine. After working for four months, the office was back to meeting its goals month after month. I worked hard for the company and its patients. In September 2019, I became funding specialist with this company in a work from home position, now I do not have to spend almost two hours driving a day, and that is more time to focus on my family and me.

Me Time

Now that my martial and work life was on track, I could take some time for myself. Since I had not been able to take a trip to see my mother in Florida since 2018, I made plans to go down for her 65th birthday, which was the week of Thanksgiving 2019. I saved up most of my vacation and, during the Thanksgiving break, was able to go and spend two weeks with my mother, which is a blessing in itself. Keep those that you love near and enjoy every moment that you can spend in their lives because you never know when it may be the last.

Daily Life

I am very thankful for being married to a man that has supported my decisions through our lives together. I am currently working as a Pampered Chef consultant and doing crafting. I still work from home, and it has taken over a good portion of my house.

While working on this chapter, my preacher came to me again and asked if I would be an Elder in my church. It took me a couple of days to think about and many prayers. Along with discussions with my husband and mother. I do not feel like I am worthy enough for such a responsibility. However, I accepted and was ordained in January 2020. Even though I know a lot of people do not believe in women leading in the church, I am ok with that. I am no longer ashamed and want to say that anyone can serve and spread God's word in the world.

You Are Strong Enough

My purpose in telling my story is not to get pity for the bad experiences in my life. My goal, no matter if you are a man or woman, is to tell you to never give up. Yes, I have had some very dark times in my life and cried myself to sleep many nights.

No matter what, God has always had a plan for me. My advice to everyone is to never be so alone that you must continue in a bad relationship or marriage like I did. I did not want to be alone. There were sometimes in my life that I had given up on God; in turn, I made myself alone without him. He will never leave you if you seek him.

Daily prayer is a struggle sometimes even for me. Nonetheless, you must find your way with him. The answer you get may not be the answer that you want; nonetheless, you have to believe in yourself and have faith to walk in the path that He has chosen for you. My story is not to tell you to go back and attempt to fix a broken marriage because everyone's life is different, and you have to do what is best for you and your path. I went back and may even still be in that up-and-down relationship if he had not of walked away from me. In the end, I had to tear myself all the way down to the ground and build myself back up to be the strong Christian woman that I am today. I am no longer afraid to show my faith to others or tell my story to help others who may be struggling.

Love is a battle, and no matter if you have been married ten days or twenty years, your faith will make that relationship stronger or provide an escape. Just remember no matter what life brings, you hold your head up high and be proud of the person you are. If you are in a relationship that has physical or verbal abuse, ask yourself is the love that you have worth all the damage that is being done to you. I could never cut the cord from my first husband because the words he told me made me feel like I would never find anyone else.

If I knew then that there were so many resources that could have helped me through my divorce, my life may be different than it is today or even stronger. Do not be ashamed to look for help; you will never know how much you need it until you get help. Keep stepping forward, for God is with you, holding your hand with every step you take. I am strong enough, and you are strong enough to.

The word of the Lord, praise be to God and all of my brothers and sisters in the world.

Amen

One of my favorite scriptures is Psalm 23. Even in my darkest moments, he has restored my soul and leads me in the path of righteousness.

Psalm 23 (KJV)

"The Lord is my shepherd; I shall not want. He maketh me to lie down in green pastures: he leadeth me beside the still waters. He restoreth my soul: he leadeth me in the paths of righteousness for his name's sake. Yea, though I walk through the valley of the shadow of death, I will fear no evil: for thou art with me; thy rod and thy staff they comfort me. Thou preparest a table before me in the presence of mine enemies: thou anointest my head with oil; my cup runneth over. Surely goodness and mercy shall follow me all the days of my life: and I will dwell in the house of the Lord forever."

Gina Erwin

authorizeddaughterofGod@gmail.com
facebook.com/GinaAuthorizedDaughterOfGod

Gina is a native New-Yorker currently residing in North Carolina. God comes first in Gina's life as she implores Godly principles in her personal and professional life. She worked in several administrative and ministries roles. Gina is a survivor of separation and divorce. She has three children and two grandchildren.

With background degrees (Bachelor's and Master's) in Business and Leadership, Gina is pursuing her Doctor of Education (EdD) in Christian/Ministry Leadership at Liberty University. Gina is an author, Senior Director at Divorce Recovery Advocates for Women, and Publishing Advocate at IGM Productions LLC.

Gina wrote her first picture book at age 15, which is published at the NY Home Instruction Library. She loves writing. She prays her writing empowers and assists others through their personal trials in life. Putting the Pieces Back Together After Adultery" is Gina's second book and her stepping out on faith in God.

Favorite Scripture

Romans 8:28-30

And we know that in all things God works for the good of those who love him, who have been called according to his purpose. For those God foreknew he also predestined to be conformed to the image of his Son, that he might be the firstborn among many brothers and sisters. And those he predestined, he also called; those he called, he also justified; those he justified, he also glorified.

Inspired Grace Media

Dedication

This chapter is first and foremost dedicated to God, who is my everything and brought me through many transformations. I would also like to dedicate this chapter to my aunty/mommy Henrietta Clarke Mealy, fondly known as Yetta, by everyone. May the words in this chapter glorify God and give recognition to the impact and life-education I was blessed with by my aunty/mommy Yetta's life, inspiration, wisdom, and love.

The Ever-Transforming Butterfly

Embrace Your Change
By: Gina Erwin

The Butterfly

The butterfly is an extraordinary creature. It begins as a caterpillar and changes into a beautiful butterfly. The change is not easy and is a process that must happen just like we change as we grow and change. Contrasting the lifecycles of butterflies and adults reveals remarkable similarities.

Just as we begin as a fertilized egg, so does the butterfly. Interestingly male butterflies have grips that are part of their abdomens, and they use them to hold the female while they impregnate her with sperm. Sound familiar? A man holds a woman in his arms. A female will lay her eggs either singularly or in multiples just as a woman can deliver one or more children. It depends on the species of butterfly as to how many eggs she will lay. Eggs are tiny and attached to the leaves of plants.

Miniature caterpillars hatch from the egg and ingest their egg for nutrition. Caterpillars eat constantly and shed several times throughout their lifecycles. They do this, so when they enter the pupa stage, they have food stored up to survive the struggle they are about to endure during their metamorphosis. A shell begins to develop under the caterpillar that will encompass it throughout the pupa stage. During the pupa stage, the caterpillar metamorphosis into a butterfly. The caterpillar breaks down, and the remains become a butterfly. Depending on the species of butterfly, this may last from as short of a time as a week or longer as a month or more. The struggle begins as the butterfly must break out of the pupa shell. The shell softens and slightly opens. The butterfly must strike the cocoon with its weak, wet, and soft wings to escape. The amazing thing here is if someone breaks the cocoon to help the butterfly to escape, the butterfly will emerge and die. The struggle of escaping the cocoon strengthens and develops the butterfly's wings and gives it the ability to fly. It must do this on its own to be able to survive. Once the butterfly escapes and its wings fully strengthen, it will lay eggs, starting the process again for new butterflies.

Much like the butterfly, we grow from an egg, then become a fetus and must be born through our mother's birth canal (or C-section) and then we live and grow into our person. The struggle the butterfly goes through is a lot like the pains, hurts, and tribulations we go through during our lives.

Egg ----- Caterpillar ----- Pupa/Chrysalis ----- Butterfly ----- Life
Egg ----- Fetus -----Baby ----- Child/Adolescence/Adult ----- Life

We have a lot in common with the butterfly. I identify with the butterfly because of its transformation and struggle. We all must transform throughout our lives. Everything we go through, good and bad, has a purpose in our transformations into the person God wants us to become and our mission within HIS plan. While somethings are rough and extremely hard, like the butterfly's metamorphosis, it all works together for our good.

"And we know that in all things God works for the good of those who love him, who have been called according to his purpose. For those God foreknew he also predestined to be conformed to the image of his Son, that he might be the firstborn

among many brothers and sisters. And those he predestined, he
also called; those he called, he also justified; those he justified,
he also glorified". ~ Romans 8:28-30

My Story

Abuse, arrest, and many other outside influences and situations are
what I have undergone and experienced. Note that I said,
"undergone". In other words, I went through those things, and they
are now past events. They do not define who I am. With God, I
was able to deal with each situation and move forward, not in fear
of being injured again, realizing I deserve to be loved and am
worthy of it. I am fearfully and wonderfully made by God (Psalm
139:14), and I have a purpose in God's plan (Romans 8:28-30).
This is my journey thus far.

Family Dynamics

Born to a single mother, raised in Harlem, New York, afflicted
with health issues during adolescence, boys were not an important
factor. Ma (the nickname I and everyone called my mother) did
what she had to for us to survive. She worked as a barmaid and in
restaurants as a waitress and a cook. Even though daddy did not
live with us as he was already in a marriage to someone else, he
was there for the important moments and major events in my life.
He loved me, and I knew it completely. I had a wonderful
relationship with his family, my grandmother, aunts, uncles, and
cousins, and still do till this day. I would have loved him to be there
every day, but I somehow understood even as a child, he could not
be there. Most importantly, the love was present, and he would
come running if his baby needed him (as you will see as we go

further). I was and will always be a daddy's girl. I was 13 when he was called home.

My maternal brother was 20 years old when I was born and had already moved out. We had a satisfactory relationship. Even though we argued, we stood by and up for each other. He constantly told me ma let me do things he never could and that I was spoiled. I also had a paternal sister and brother by my father. They, too, were grown and not a big part of my life. My sister and I wrote and phoned each other occasionally as we lived on opposite sides of the world. All contact with my paternal brother ended after my father died. (I am overjoyed to announce my paternal brother, and I have reunited while I was penning this chapter). My paternal sister and I remained in contact until she was called home the week after my mother passed. I lived the life of an only child. My mother was my world after daddy passed. My mother passed when I was nineteen. At this very moment and forever, I will miss and love them both.

Growing Up

I do not have a lot of young childhood memories. I remember some happy moments with family members during holidays, birthday parties, and special events. The most memorable individuals are of my Godparents, Ruth and Teddy, neighbors like Mrs. Smith, Ms. Lucy, and other elders that lived in the building and looked out for me when ma was working. God continuously placed the people I needed around me.

I have no problem remembering the tough times. I started having a lot of pain and problems with both of my legs during adolescence (10+) and had two major surgeries. I woke up one morning and tried to walk to the bathroom and could not put any weight on my right leg. Ma took me to the emergency room, where they admitted

me for surgery. The doctors diagnosed me with a slipped epiphysis of the right hip. In layman's terms, that means the ball and socket bones in my hip and thigh separated. At that time, this was new to the medical community. They knew what the problem was but was not aware of the long-term effects. The doctors went in and pinned the bones back together. The doctors did not realize that my bone had rotated, and when they pinned it back in place, my leg was now rotated 90 degrees outward. I developed an infection following the surgery, and they wanted to go back in to collect the infection (for research), break the bones, reset them, and put a plate in my hip. Ma and I declined as I had begun walking again even while yet in a cast.

Daddy to the rescue! Daddy was a policeman and busy. When I needed him, he came and did whatever was required. Daddy came and took me to a specialist who explained I would require hip replacement later in life. Since hip replacements only lasted approximately 20 years before necessitating replacement, we should leave it alone for now, since I could walk without pain. During that same visit, the specialist also found that my left knee was rotating outward, and I required immediate surgery to correct it before it became a problem. Daddy arranged for the surgery at one of the major hospitals in New York. The specialist placed three temporary pins through my lower left leg. They stuck out each side like the bolts in Frankenstein's head. After a few months, the specialist removed the pins during an office visit. He numbed my leg, twisted them with a tool, and pulled them out. I had to use crutches, receive homeschooling, and stay home for a while.

When Daddy Left

As always, daddy came and made things right. He would fill the Christmas tree with dolls, toys, and other gifts for Christmas. He attended every birthday party, most major events, and always came to check on me when I was sick. He would take me to see grandma Bea, and I would sit in her window with grandpa looking out at people going back and forth in busy New York City. He would take me to see my paternal aunts, uncles, cousins, and other family members. He may not have lived in the same home with me, yet we occupied each other's hearts and minds.

I still can remember the phone ringing. I answered it, and it was aunty/mommy Yetta. She asked to speak with ma and told me she loved me and would see me soon. I knew by the sound of her voice something was wrong, and something inside of me said daddy was dead. Unfortunately, I was right. Daddy had died. He was called home to be with God. I was still on crutches as we attended the funeral. I saw my paternal family and spent time with them as we said our farewells to daddy. Even now, I remember the sounds of the trumpets and the guns as they did a three-gun salute. Just like that, in an instant, my daddy was gone.

Teenage Years

After two surgeries, physical therapy, the loss of my father, I was able to return to school, and normal everyday events. I realized all my girlfriends now had boyfriends, all except for me, the girl with the limp. One of the nicknames given to me by my peers back then was "weeble-wobbles". It did negatively faze me. However, once I embraced the title and laughed about it, it got easier. God constantly gave me friends that are awesome and supportive, so a lot of things did not damage me as awfully as they would have if I did not have a supportive peer system (male and female). I am still friends with many of them including my two junior high school sisters Kimi and Kioka (The Three Stooges- as we were nicknamed by our Dean Silkowitz).

The boys thought I walked funny and were not paying me much attention, but the older grown men were. Today, as I pen these words, I know it was not an appropriate thing, and I was being taken advantage of. At the time, I adored the attention, and it felt awesome. I was influenced by a few and fell for one. That was when I learned what the power of love comprises. When you love someone, you are willing to do anything, even if it is wrong or demoralizing. It is as if your heart overrules your brain, and you just act without thinking. You want the person to feel the power of the love you have for them, and you are willing to do anything to prove that love.

Mr. Tall & Handsome

I was 15 years old (almost 16), in the 12th grade, and on the way to graduating high school six months early. Right before I turned 16, my mother's friend and neighbor came to introduce us to her son. He was so tall, handsome, and seemed to be a virtuous person. I was on the loveseat doing homework, and he told me to keep up with my schoolwork because it was important. A few weeks later, I was celebrating my 16th birthday. My mother allowed us to utilize the empty apartment next to ours to have a large open space for my party. My friends and I laughed, danced, and had a great time that night. What I thought at that time was the best present of the evening, truly was not.

I was in the building hallway with some friends cooling off from dancing, and Mr. Tall and Handsome was coming down the stairs from his mother's apartment. He asked what we were doing, and I explained it was my 16th birthday. He wished me a happy birthday and kissed me smack dab on the lips. To say the least, I was mesmerized. He said, "Happy Birthday Hot Lips," slipped me a piece of paper with his phone number written on it, turned smiling, proceeded down the stairs, and left the building. In my daze, I hung over the banister and watched him descend each of the five flights of the stair until he was gone. I returned to my party and had a great time, now feeling awesome due to my birthday encounter. I knew he was older, but that did not deter me at all. That was just the beginning of my journey, searching for the love of a man. This would not be the last encounter with Mr. Tall and Handsome. The next encounter came sooner than I anticipated.

I had never skipped school in my entire existence and was always considered a goody-two-shoes. One morning when I was on my way to school and running late, a friend, Antonio, saw me and asked me to hang out with him. I wanted to because I had always thought he was a cutie-pie. However, something terrible happened to another girl in the block, and some said he was involved. I regrettably explained I had to go. After arriving too late to be admitted to the first period, a friend, Nessa, and I decided to skip school. We went to her house, which was coincidentally across the park from Mr. Tall and Handsome's apartment.

After hanging out with Nessa for a while, I called Mr. Tall and Handsome and was invited over. I knew that I more than likely would no longer be a virgin after this. I still went, nervous yet excited because finally, I believed I was going to obtain my very own man. I reveled in the fact that he was not a boy, he could protect me, and he was going to become mine. I did lose my virginity that day, completely fell for him, and gave into him 100%.

Unbeknownst to me, I 100% became his, but he would never be mine. I was 16, and for his protection, he would never acknowledge me as his lady, even if he considered me that. If caught with me, 31-year-old Mr. Tall and Handsome would be liable for statutory rape.

Secondly, I soon learned that his heart belonged to someone else, the mother of his firstborn child. Due to her no longer choosing to be in a relationship with him, he dated other women, not caring for them or me. One day, as I was sitting in his living room with him and his daughter, her mother unlocked the door using her own set of keys and entered. We politely said hi to each other. They left me in the living room and went into the bedroom to talk. They exited the room, and she left with their daughter.

Being around their daughter, I came to admire her very much and still do today. She was beautiful and full of essence. I used to pick their daughter up from school and take her to her grandmother's or home. Her mother and I became acquainted and were continually respectful of each other, never talking about our relationships with Mr. Tall and Handsome. I looked up to her, not just because she consumed his heart, also because of the way she carried herself. She constantly dressed beautifully, was respectful, and courteous. She was the type of woman I wanted to be. Even in my mess, God was providing wisdom.

Mr. Tall and Handsome became my obsession, and I became his puppet. Anything he asked me to do, I would do. When he wanted me physically, I was onboard and obliged. It did not matter where we were; I consented to his wishes. It was not just sexual submission. My submission was absolute. One day he told me he had done some work for the superintendent of the building and was going to be paid by check. He explained that he lost his ID and could not get the checked cashed. He asked if the superintendent put the check-in my name could I get it cashed. I was working part-time at a pre-school, so I had access to check cashing at the neighborhood grocery store. I told him, yes, and he had the superintendent make the check out to me. This happened a few more times. A few months and six to seven checks later, all was fine. I had no idea what I had gotten myself involved in. I would soon find out.

My mother told and asked me all in the same sentence that I was pregnant. She had dreamt of fish, and that was her dream translated. Do not mock the beliefs and wisdom of your elders. I was pregnant. I felt happy and scared. It happened around my 17th birthday (December). I do not remember if I celebrated my 17th birthday or not because, at the time, it was all about him. Mr. Tall and Handsome did not want me to keep the baby. It proved that he committed statutory rape even if I willingly allowed it. Later he explained that this might be the son he always wanted and told me not to have an abortion. I was not going to have an abortion in the first place. If he had persisted, I planned to move down south with my mother's family, if necessary, to keep from having an abortion. For my baby's existence, I took a stand against his original wishes. We were having a baby.

When I was about two months pregnant, one Sunday morning returning to my mother's house, two detectives stopped me and arrested me for forgery and grand larceny. The checks I had cashed for him were erroneous. I learned years later from a mutual friend of ours, Mr. Tall and Handsome, found a ledger containing the checks in a garbage can outside of a bank that had shut down.

The year 1984 started on a bad foot. I was pregnant and facing jail time. After spending the night in jail, I attended my arraignment (first court appearance). I watched my mother march into the courtroom with at least four other people. I was already feeling ashamed for being arrested, and ma was giving me an audience. The judge released me on my own recognizance and issued a new court date for trial. The court assigned me a court-appointed lawyer. After going home, getting cleaned up and eating, I excitedly was ready to see Mr. Tall and Handsome (dumb in love). When I got there, he laughed about the whole thing and

jokingly called me a jailbird. I was so happy to be home and be with him I paid it no mind. Love was clouding my thinking and my judgment. He only wanted to know if I told them he had given me the checks. That should have woken me up, but it did not. I had to pay restitution of most of the money and remain out of trouble for a year. If I could do that, all the charges would eventually be expunged from my record. I did that all on my own, and the situation was never discussed between him and me again.

I thought that was the worst that could happen. Was I wrong! Now, I was about to see the not so sweet side of Mr. Tall and Handsome. He was in a fight, and I tried to stop him. I was thrown up against the wall and immediately fled the apartment with the fight intensifying, afraid of getting physically harmed (I was pregnant). I did not know what was going to happen. A day later he called me and told me to come to his place. I was scared because I did not know what occurred after I left. The house was clean, and all looked fine. I did not question any of the situations that had occurred.

A noticeably short time after this, Mr. Tall and Handsome was arrested on other charges. I trudged through ice and snow, pregnant, to visit him regularly. He called one day because I had not come. There were about six inches of snow on the ground. The next day, Gina, young dumb and full..., went to the jail to see her man.

In August 1984, I delivered a seven-pound, twelve-ounce baby boy by cesarean section while Mr. Tall and Handsome continued his incarceration. His daughter's mom called me at the hospital to see how I was. After I told her the baby's name, she chuckled. I knew the name alone assured her it was his baby.

A few months later he was released, he moved in with his grandmother, right around the corner. It was no longer the same.

One night, I left my son with my mother and met him outside of my building. After walking to and having sex with him in the park, he got high. As we were walking out of the park, he strangled me to the point of unconsciousness. I came to as he was picking me up off the ground. He stated I was faking. Then, he took my keys and left me. He went to my house and entered to see the baby. Scared, after he left, my mother called his grandmother to see if she knew where I was and why he had my keys. After his grandmother (the only person he respected and listened to) chastised him, he came back around the corner and attacked my mother, severely. My mother did not press charges because she and his grandmother were close friends. She did not want his grandmother to have to go through it with him.

My mother's beating was enough to finally wake me up and begin to distance myself from him. That angered him. He caught me in the building next to mine, waiting for my girlfriend to come downstairs. He grabbed me by the neck and told me if he did not get to see his son, he would kill me. I obtained an order of protection, and he was served by New York's Finest as we called the police back then. He stayed away up until he realized I was seeing someone else. Friends called and told me he began walking up and down the street ranting about how I better get downstairs and see him and not be spending time with anyone else. He even followed us to a bar one night and began drinking and talking to my new guy and me. He eventually went back to jail, and it was quiet for a long while.

I was now 17, about to turn 18, I had my first child, first sexual experience, my first taste of abuse, first arrest, first heartbreak, and many more firsts. I had been lied to, emotionally and physically abused, strangled to the point of unconsciousness, arrested, and wounded deep in my heart. Along with my firsts came shame and the acknowledgment that my loved ones were extremely disappointed by some of my choices and actions. They let me know it too. Remarks were made, and the way some had always treated me became tempered with distrust and disappointment. All except for one person.

My Second Mother

My aunty/mommy Yetta (as I fondly call her) and my dad's family were the only ones who never changed or criticized my past decisions. She always gave me unconditional love and encouraged me to keep moving forward, trusting God, and doing my best at any and everything I set my hands to do. She will forever be one of the strongest women in my life. She has been my aunt, friend, teacher, advisor (spiritually and otherwise), confidant, go-to, and so much more. She willingly stepped in the role of mother after my mother passed when I was 20 years old and has been there for me at every moment since.

My aunty/mommy Yetta was an extraordinary woman. She was special, independent, loving, humble, and a woman of God. She placed God first and foremost in her existence. She is egocentric and does not run to make changes when technology offers it. She maintained a regular house phone without a three-way calling or any of the other accessories offered today. If she were on the phone when you called, you would get a busy signal (in the 21st century lol). She tried to learn computers, but they just do not fit into her busy schedule. Retired, she volunteered at the veteran's hospital near her home regularly. She would help anyone in need if she can. She has the biggest heart I have ever seen anyone to possess. Astrology was her specialty. She began teaching me, but our distance impeded the process. She would do charts seeking the compatibility of my potential male companions, and her information continually was on point. It was funny because my youngest daughter started asking me to ask aunty/mommy Yetta whether she was compatible with or should date certain young men she encountered. My aunty/mommy Yetta would not hesitate to do charts for her as well.

Some would say she was different, and I concur. She thrived and related on a higher level. Her connection with God and the universe was powerful and enlightening. She did not go to doctors or take prescription medicines. She embraced herbal and holistic remedies while regularly walking miles every day. She fasted regularly and gave everything to God. I often jokingly asked her for her secrets and the location of the fountain of youth she tapped. She would laugh and always give glory to God.

She periodically sent me what she called "ice cream money". What is "ice cream money"? It is $20 for when life gets you down, and you feel like "screaming". You are to spend it on ice cream or something that will lift your spirits. Each time she sent it I was at that point. She just seemed to know when to send it, via her intuition and our connection. She knew that, and she also called me when I had to make major decisions. She would call me and say something that answered all my dilemmas and decision-making choices. We told each other we loved the other, multiple times throughout our calls. We would catch up on what was going on and discuss our futures. She was my rock, spiritual advisor, and go-to authority, second to no one other than God Himself.

At 92 years young, she continued to live the way she desired and saw fit (even driving). She looked 50 years old and nowhere near her true age. She was so beautiful and possessed a glowing redbone complexion, that reminds me of how the Bible describes Moses after being on the mountain with God (Exodus 34:29). She was and will forever be the epitome of love and how God wants us to be. I pray I am half the woman she was.

As I penned this chapter, she too has been called home after having a stroke. I am saddened and overwhelmed with grief. Due to the COVID-19 pandemic, I could not go to see her. I will continue to pray and trust God through this as she has always taught me to. I can hear her saying, "Don't cry for me, I am home with God, my parents, siblings, and treasured ones. I am at peace. Be happy for me". I know she will forever be with me eternally guiding me, only now from above. I now must take all she taught me and teach it to our next generations. She forever lives on in my heart.

God Makes His Presence Known

As a child, I knew God existed and prayed to HIM every night. I knew HE could hear, protect, guide, and was eternally with me. I do not know where my belief and faith came from because ma did not go to church and rarely spoke of God. My Godmother Ruth did take me to the Catholic church across the street to light candles and pray. She taught me the "Now I Lay Me Down to Sleep" and the "Lord's Prayer". We would also sit on the fire-escape on the weekends and watch the beautiful weddings taking place at the church. Other than that, my exposure to church was minimal and limited.

The one-man my mother dated that I considered a father figure, Alphonso, whom I called dad, was a Deacon and sang in a gospel choir. We would go with him to church sometimes and to his performances. Even after ma and he broke up, I periodically attended his church and spoke to him regularly. After moving out of NY, we stayed in touch until he, too, was called home.

My aunty/mommy Yetta continuously told me how to pray and who God is. She taught me about fasting and many other aspects of prayer and worship. Repeatedly, God made sure I encountered the people that kept me close to HIM including ma and Alphonso.

Second Try at Love

While I did embrace God and prayed to HIM, I did not have a clue about forgiveness and how unforgiveness impeded my journey. I went on running from one love to another, searching for happiness and my happily ever after. When running from Mr. Tall and Handsome, the man I loved, believed was my forever, created a son with, and was physically traumatized by, I embraced the fairytale sagas we are taught from childhood. I ran from him straight into the arms of a man whom I trusted would protect, love, and provide my fairytale ending.

At 18, I ran from the man I thought would be the love of my life, my first love, I started looking for something I already had in God. I did not comprehend that all I required, and will ever require, is God. I thought I needed a man. My next relationship was with Alex, never did he physically harm me. He gave me everything I thought I needed and wanted. He did this to a fault, forsaking essentials to provide unnecessary desires I believed I should have. I could see a dress or item I fancied and wanted, and he would get it even if it meant spending the rent money to do so. My hands and body were full of jewelry and clothes I said I liked when we were out together. I knew we should not be spending money on these items because we had bills to pay. Both of us just went along, continuing this type of behavior.

After I started dating him, I moved out of my mother's apartment to the one across the hall. He began living with me and treating my son like he was his. We celebrated my 19th birthday with a huge get-together. Life seemed pleasant, and I stopped looking over my shoulder. Mr. Tall and handsome was in jail, and I was at peace.

We had friends, and we both were working and maintaining our home. The fairytale saga soon came to a halt. We started arguing, and he would leave and go to his mother's and stay there for days at a time. This went on periodically, and when we reunited, everything would be okay until the next time.

I suffered three miscarriages (two sets of twins and one baby). A few months after the miscarriages, my mother dreamt of fish once again. I was pregnant with his first and my second child so, we tried to get it right. It was a difficult pregnancy. I suffered from major migraines and horrible nausea. I would crave food, and he would get it, and after eating it, I would throw it right back up. I had to stop working during my fourth month of pregnancy. Alex took care of me and tried to make sure I had everything I desired. After my sixth month of pregnancy, the arguments started again. One day after our usual separations, he returned from his mother's place and asked me to marry him. My mother adored him, and despite the arguments, I knew he was a suitable man. I was about to have his baby, and I knew he treasured me despite the petty arguments. I cannot even remember what caused them. We decided to do what was best for us and our family. We were married three weeks later.

The wedding took place in the pre-school classroom I taught in and the reception in the downstairs kitchen and dining area. My family attended while his mother and brother did not. His mother and I got along well until marriage entered the picture. Suddenly, she considered me the wicked witch and did not want him to marry me. My boss gave me away. Two of my co-workers and two of my 'inherited' sisters (not blood but sisters in all other aspects) were my bride's maids and matron of honor. It was a beautiful day and event. The reception moved to my apartment after the elders left and lasted two days. It was a joyous time even though I was eight months pregnant and toting around a belly.

In the delivery room (cesarean section), something went horribly wrong. Instead of numbing me from the waist down, I was numbed from the head down. The doctor asked me if I felt something in my legs, and as I said yes, I felt a pain in my head. The next thing I remember is waking up in the operating room with the doctor holding a tumor the size of a navel orange, telling me they had to remove it and one of my ovaries during the procedure. I could remember hearing my baby crying, and I really could not stand having the respirator in my throat. The anesthesiologist removed the respirator, and after catching my breath, I asked where my baby was. They explained she was in the nursery and that I could see her soon. They were more worried about the fact I had not regained any feeling in my legs at that point.

Finally, I was taken to my room and united with my beautiful six-pound twelve-and-a-half-ounce baby girl. I was overjoyed. I finally had my little girl. She was healthy, and all was right with the world. I finally regained the feeling in my legs the next day. No one seems to know what went wrong. The tumor was benign, and I went home with my baby girl.

Life went well for a while. We were both working, parenting, and partying with friends after the kids went to bed. I started playing spades and bid whist outside of the apartment building into the wee hours of the morning. I also initiated an emotional relationship with a married guy at my place of employment. It was not sexual until the very end, although it was wrong in all aspects. We went places together, had fun, dined, went to amusement parks, talked, laughed, and had an amazing time together. It was something I was no longer getting from Alex, and I realized it too late. My "friend" ended up moving out of New York, and the relationship ended with his departure. Shortly after that loss, and it was a painful loss, even though it was wrong, I lost my mother.

Ma Left Me

My mother (biological), Ma, had an addiction to alcohol, and it was slowly killing her. Once she stopped working, all she did was sit in her chair and drink. Living across the hall from her allowed me to cook for her and make sure she was okay daily. Many days I would find her food in the trash as she did not have a sound appetite and would eat small amounts. She would cook every so often when she had a taste for something. Mostly it was alcohol and television. She had a special bond with my firstborn (son). The first two years of his life he lived with her even after I moved across the hall. While they were inseparable, after her getting sick, I would only let him sit with her during the day and come to sleep in my apartment at night. I feared him waking up and her not being alive.

One morning Alex went to see if ma was hungry. I was cooking breakfast. He came back across the hall and said she did not want anything. Around lunchtime, two of my maternal aunts came to see ma. I unlocked the door and let them in. Moments later, they came back, screaming that ma was not responding. I called an ambulance and was later told ma had pneumonia, was in a coma, and on a respirator. I would visit her daily and talk to her, praying she could hear me and recover. I would ask her to move for me, and finally, she moved her foot. I told the nurses and doctor, but they said it was most likely involuntary. The next day she emerged out of the comma. She pulled out her respirator tube, essentially spreading pneumonia to the other lung. A few days later, ma was gone.

I was 20 years old and married with children, I still was not ready to lose my mother. It was hard holding it together. I had to plan the funeral, and I even gave the eulogy. To this day, I know God gave me the strength and courage to get through. One friend told me that he did not know what to say but just know that he was there if I needed him. This remark meant the world to me. It meant so much more than the people saying she was in a better place, they were sorry, and it would get better with time. Truthfully, it does not get better with time. You just learn how to keep moving forward. The loss is eternally there.

North Carolina & A Miracle

Our marriage continued, and we eventually relocated to North Carolina, wanting better surroundings for us and our children. We lived with my maternal brother and his family, who had moved there a couple of years earlier. We were doing fine, and once we moved to our own house, everything improved. We attended church regularly, and Alex worked at the local grocery store. Our kids were growing up, and all seemed okay. Nothing is perfect, but we were in a wonderful space.

Ten years late I got sick and thought it was a stomach virus. After going to the doctor, she informed me that I was pregnant. Really??? I now believed that God has an awesome sense of humor. Especially since I had only one ovary after the last c-section. By this time, my children were 15 and 17. I was thinking about vacations and cruises, not parenting again, but I was overjoyed. Alex seemed to be in shock and did not react. The miracle of my conceiving is a long story, and I will save it for another book. To shorten it, I will tell you, it was a difficult pregnancy, and there were many signs that God was walking with me, before, during, and afterwards. I gave birth to a beautiful eight-pound baby girl. I did not know then, but I later understood God had a plan.

The End of My Marriage

My middle child (daughter) left for college, and my firstborn (son) got his own place. Our marriage continued but was no longer prosperous. We had separate bedrooms and barely talked and interacted. I focused on my youngest daughter, hoping it would change. It did not, and when my youngest (daughter) was six, it all finally fell apart.

I was teaching Sunday school and the youth bible study group. I also was the pastor's assistant and secretary. My pastor taught me so much about God, and my relationship with HIM just increased. Alex was a deacon in the church and led the Sunday youth ministry. If you looked at us in public, you would think we had a great relationship. Behind closed doors, that was not the case. We were two people living as roommates and putting on a show for others. The intimacy was never totally what I would call extraordinary, but it worked until it was totally null and void.

In public, we were a loving husband and wife duo. Upon returning home, he went to his room, and I went to the room I shared with my youngest daughter. I believed by ignoring the painful truth, the situation would somehow fix itself, or God would miraculously fix it. I thought I was doing what was best for my daughter (a two-parent home). I was wrong. The truth slapped me into reality. My husband was mentally checked out of the whole situation, and everything was at a standstill.

One day my youngest daughter (six years old) walked up to me and started crying. When I asked her what was wrong, she explained she did not know and that she was just incredibly sad. At that moment, I realized the unhappiness within the household was running over into her and negatively affecting her. She was feeling the breakdown between her parents and it was depressing her. I knew things had to change right then and there.

I took a thorough look in the mirror and did not like the woman looking back at me. I was overweight, unhappy, and miserable. I began working on myself, hoping that fixing myself would somehow assist in correcting my marriage. I started going to a gym and joined a nutrition-based weight loss group. My daughter would go with me when she was not in school. It became a regimen, and I searched to find myself, the me that had been bogged down under my roles as wife, homemaker, employee, church leader, and mother. I lost 80 pounds and started to see my existence a lot differently. I was happy to go out in public without having to utilize a wheelchair, and once again, compliments came from the male species. I still walked with a limp, but as my self-confidence increased it was not a factor.

One night, I was asked by my husband if I still loved him. I took some time to respond because although I knew the answer, I never wanted to aggrieve him. I calmly explained that I loved him and permanently would, but that I was no longer in love with him and severely unhappy with the union we shared. A lot of disappointment, wrong attitudes, poor decisions, and chaos followed. Ultimately, he left the state and moved in with a family member. We each moved on in our separate ways. We talked and were cordial because of our love for our children and the continued raising of our youngest daughter, who was only six years old. I had to move also because I could not handle the mortgage on the house we were purchasing together.

I chose to move to another city because I was tired of running into people asking questions about the situation. Again, I was running without realizing it. I launched a new dating resolve, met many prospective partners, and made some substandard decisions before trying to make it work out with one in the city I now resided.

He treated me well and did the manly things I needed around the house. However, my physical condition was a source of contention for him. I walked with a limp and was experiencing overactive nerves, which made me tremor regularly. These were physical disabilities that I had no power over. It afflicted me deep inside that he could not see past them. When we were alone, it was all enjoyable, but he did not want the world to know I was his lady. I also found out later he was also seeing another woman in the next town over. I masked the pain with a smile, pretended I was unaware and kept believing it would get better. I realized how some men looked at me, and it affected my self-confidence. My confidence took a huge nose-dive, and again, the search to be complete continued.

Real Love at Last???

By now, my self-confidence was failing, and I was tired of the pain that seemed to eventually present itself into my relationships. While yet holding on to the man cheating on me and embarrassed to be seen with me, I met a man online who showed interest in me and wanted to talk via the phone. Tired of rejection due to my flaws and a confidence level of 25%, I bluntly told him that if he was in search of a trophy woman on his arm that I was not her. He responded by saying I was beautiful and asked me what I thought was wrong with me. I gave him the list of flaws presented to me by other men and my personal beliefs. He asked, "Is that all?" and waited for my response. In shock, I did not know how to respond. The conversation finally continued with us talking about what we wanted from a relationship and his declaration that he was going to make me fall in love with him. He did that. After a few months of constant phone calls, I picked him up for what was supposed to be a weekend visit to get to know each other that did not end for seven years. When I arrived at his cousin's house to pick him up, she explained he had taken her daughter down the street to the park and would be right back. Moments later, he walked in, bent down, gently held my face in his hand, and kissed me. I was done. At that moment, I knew how Sleeping Beauty must have felt when Prince Charming kissed and awoke her. We talked for a while with his cousin and then left for my place. I said nothing as we drove home. I was infatuated and starstruck. After arriving home, my daughter soon returned from school. He was so loving and attentive to not just me but my daughter as well. As our relationship grew, she started to call him daddy (her desire, not mine). The guy I was trying to hold onto that made my self-confidence drop was eventually pushed out of the picture. Once again, I was in fairytale land. I should have known better by now. In my lifetime, I had realized that fairytales are just that, tales. However, deep within my soul, I wanted to believe I could have a fairytale ending, no matter how strong my mind kept saying beware.

My love for him became an addiction. I pushed God to the side and found myself only praying to God when he required something. I lost myself in him and the relationship we were building. It felt satisfying being loved for who I was and not what someone wanted me to be, so much that I did not even realize what I was doing until it was too late. I never felt the way he made me feel. I trusted him and became blind to what was happening.

I found out most of what he told me, in the beginning, was lies mixed with minimal truths. He was running from the law, did not own a vehicle (in the shop), and had no place of his own. The friends he made were into things I was not. They enjoyed drinking and drugs regularly. I am not inexperienced or a prude, I would take a drink from time to time and tried my share of drugs back in the day. However, I was a mother and had too many responsibilities to party like that any longer. After my mother's addiction to alcohol, I kind of lost the taste for it and only drank one or two drinks on occasion.

Because of his actions, he spent a couple of short periods in jail. One of those periods was for slapping me so hard; my face looked as if I scraped it on concrete. He apologized repeatedly and admitted that he was high (which I knew). I forgave him and explained if he ever put his hands on me again, I would leave him, and he would never see me again. He knew I meant it because it was the first time, I did not allow his words to back me down and give in.

Once all the drama and chaos were over, and he returned home, we moved back to the town I had fled from two years earlier, where my son and his family were. It was supposed to be a new beginning, and we were happy for a while. One thing I can say is the man loved me in his own way. I believe that in his concept of love, I was the true love of his life. If he did not love me, he deserves an academy award. I had health issues and had to have major surgery on the discs in my neck (collapsing/crushing my spinal cord). To say the least, I was terrified. I remember the night before the surgery, he held me in his arms and prayed to God asking HIM to take the situation off me and place it on him. I loved him even more as he spoke those words to God. He never left my side during the surgery process and slept in the reclining chair in my room right next to me. He fed me, and once back home, he took care of me as if I were a baby.

Two years later, I had hip replacement surgery, and though he took care of me, his behavior while I was in the hospital was not usual. His commitment was not as strong as it was during my neck surgery a year earlier. He left the hospital this time to go hang out with his family and old friends. He returned, looking like he had partied to the hilt. I was not his primary concern, and I knew it. I was too exhausted from the surgery and rehabilitation to protest.

New friends entered the picture, and his behavior changed. He was doing drugs, and I knew it. After telling him I was leaving him, he swore he would get it together and asked me to marry him. He promised that he would be the husband I deserved, and everything would be great moving forward. Foolishly, I married him. I knew better, but I cherished him so much and wanted nothing more than to be his wife.

After getting married, it was enjoyable for a while, with minor disagreements, but it did not last. A year and a half later, it all went to hell. We moved to a better house with more room and much better accommodations. That did not help. I began seeing a darker side of him that I did not like at all. I knew he was cheating. However, I had no proof good enough to dismiss his words of explanation and denial. Soon he began staying out late or all night. I started to retaliate by yelling and saying things that I thought would wake him up and get it right. The things I thought were okay to say and scream at him, upset him, and only made the situation worse. I even stopped being intimate with him for fear of catching something and believing it would force him to change. While my actions protected me physically, they impeded any healing that could be applied going forward and became what he considered a catalyst and motivation for him to keep doing what he was doing. It became crazy, intolerable, and dangerous. Finally, my daughter and I packed up, put our stuff into storage, and moved in with my son and his family.

After leaving, it got worse than anyone could ever imagine. He called me, and during the conversation, I referenced his girlfriend that he was cheating on me with. He had told me while I was packing to leave that it was okay, he had a new girlfriend that would take care of him. Initially, I believed he was just lying to get a reaction out of me. To my utter surprise, she got on the phone and talked much trash to me about my husband. When I retaliated, yelling some very unGodly things, called her everything but a child of God, and threatened to sue her for alienation of affection, my husband hung up the phone. When he called back, he told me I should not disrespect her like that. After saying more unGodly words to him, I hung up and commenced screaming out to God. The pain I felt in my heart was devastating. I followed that up by drinking brandy and contemplating how to punish him as he had just mentally afflicted me. Pain became anger, anger turned to vengeance, and amid it all, I wanted to die. I did not want to feel the pain anymore. I contemplated on swallowing a whole bottle of pills and just going to sleep and never deal with the pain again.

As I was going through all of this, my youngest daughter came in from school with my daughter-in-law (coming from picking up my grandchildren) to find me a blubbering, intoxicated mess. They took the liquor away from me. My daughter held me in her arms and told me it was going to be okay. Here my beautiful youngest daughter, now 16-years old, was holding and consoling me, something I should have been doing for her. She is part of God's plan, and I now realized her purpose within HIS plan. Her existence was ordained by God to save me and do so much more.

My best friend called and prayed over me as she did through this whole process. I finally laid down and fell asleep. Upon waking in the middle of the night, the pain was still there and so overwhelmingly intense. I screamed internally, not to wake anyone in the house. I cried and again thought that death would be better than what I was feeling. In my mind, I saw my daughter's face and realized my death would only torment her and that she needed me. I also knew that it would grieve my two other children and disappoint God, so the idea of suicide was dismissed from my agenda thankfully.

The pain remained, and it would change in intensity without any warning. Thoughts would permeate my mind, a song would play, and an actor or actress would say something, and I would again fall to pieces. Highs and lows entered my being with no warning and could not be stopped.

My daughter-in-law and I had been through our share of ups and downs, but we had grown to a proficient place with each other. We had loved and disliked each other on different occasions. We had found our way back to loving, and I was overjoyed about that. She is a beautiful woman that makes my son happy and gave birth to my grandchildren. I thank God for her. She came into my room, and boldly stated, "Ma, you are a strong woman of God, you hold your own, and never give up. I have never seen you like this. I need you to fight and come back to us!". The words were like an awakening and jarred my mind back to reality. Even now, I can see and hear my daughter-in-law as she spoke those words to me, awakening the fight in me once again. I will forever love her for loving me enough to be there for me when I needed her the most.

My son wanted me to be strong, move on, and he, of course, wanted to go after my husband because he hurt me. My son has forever been my protector and has no problem defending the honor of his mother. I had to explain that it was not what was needed. I knew I needed to get past it and heal. I also knew I needed God and to fix my relationship with HIM.

I had an awesome set of people in my corner, reassuring, loving, and praying with, over, and for me. About a year before all this God sent me a best friend and sister. She prayed over me daily, reassured me I could get through this, and advised me as she had gone through similar and had also contemplated suicide. I knew when we met; there was something special about her. I now know that she is a gift and blessing from God, as HE already knew I would need her. Having a reliable support system is essential. I thank God for my awesome support system. They were there for me, kept me pushing forward and closer to God where I desperately craved to return to. While I knew I needed to heal and had an awesome support system, I had no clue that forgiveness was the way to heal. I could not heal or move forward if I did not forgive.

The Freedom of Forgiveness & God's Love

Every experience that I have written about never once did you hear me say anything about closure or forgiveness. That is because I blindly moved forward searching for validity and happiness in man and not God. I did not forgive any of the men that had previously grieved me. I harnessed my pain, and it turned to anger, raunchy behavior, and continuous wrong choices. Life's lessons taught me that great injustices happen to us all, and all involved must be forgiven. I have learned this means you and everyone involved.

Forgiveness does not mean you must continue dealing with them, but God's word says you must forgive and love them. You can love them from a distance. Loving someone means you pray for them, want the best for them (with or without you in their lives), wish them no harm, and hold no ill-will towards them. I said love, not be best friends. In forgiving others, let the past go, so it does not keep reentering your thoughts and causing discord. Yes, we all are harmed by actions, lack of actions, and involvement in painful situations. Just know, you must forgive them because God requires it, they need it, it will clear you, and you must forgive to be forgiven.

When we hold onto grudges and do not forgive, it empowers the individuals we are upset with and gives them a hold on us they should not have. Have you ever been upset with someone, run into them, or even thought about them, and your whole mood changes? Did the memory take you from contentment to being upset? No one should have that type of control or affect over you except for God. Forgiveness and giving it to God allows you to free yourself. You release yourself from the burden of holding a grudge and being unforgiving, while gaining God's approval and the ability to be forgiven.

It happened and cannot be undone, no matter what you do. You are not the judge or jury; God is. When you forgive, you appropriately deal with the situation in a Godly manner, not out of spite or any other inappropriate emotions. Forgive and free yourself. Move forward in the purpose God has for you, not allowing your journey to be impeded by unforgiveness.

I went from one relationship to the next, not dealing with my damaged feelings and believing the opinions of the men that I looked to for validation. I never forgave anyone. I just kept going with those emotions building and wreaking havoc on my mind, body, spirit, and soul. I could not understand why I kept getting hurt and wondered what I was doing wrong. As I had closed myself off from God, I had lost my guidance and was operating outside of the spirit.

Once I started to call out and pray to God, things began to get clear. I realized some important facts:

- Love is essential (1 Corinthians 13:1-3)
- Love does not hurt anyone – people do (1 Corinthians 13:4-8)
- Everyone is imperfect (Romans 3:21-24)
- People cause pain on others intentionally and unintentionally (Psalm 19:12; Luke 23:24)

- God's love is the only perfect love (1 John 4:9-11)
- We will be afflicted throughout our journeys (1 Peter 5:8-9)
- What we do with and how we handle the hurt decides our outcomes (Galatians 6:7-10)
- We must forgive because God requires us to (Matthew 18: 21-22)
- We must forgive ourselves and others (Ephesians 4:31-32)
- We must forgive to heal (Micah 7:18-19)
- We must forgive to be forgiven (Matthew 6:14-15)
- We must forgive to be free (Isaiah 1:18)
- We must forgive to love again (Luke 7:47-50)
- God created women to love men, help men, and they are a part of men (rib) making a women's desire to be with a man inherent (Genesis 2:18,21-24, 3:16)

Self-Forgiveness

Self-forgiveness comes first. You may be asking yourself, "Why did I do that?" "What is wrong with me?" "Was I not worthy enough?" or "What could I have done differently?". Feeling responsible or blaming yourself is normal. You must forgive yourself for any responsibility you have placed on yourself and ask God to forgive you as well. Once you sincerely ask God to forgive you, HE does. It is you that must let it go. You are not perfect, and you have and will make mistakes. **IT IS NOT YOUR FAULT!** It happened, and now it is time to face it and move forward. You cannot move forward until you forgive yourself.

Self-forgiveness is more laborious than forgiving others. We are harder on ourselves than anyone else. It starts with you. You are a child of God, loved by HIM, and you can overcome all things and situations with HIS help. Once you have forgiven yourself for everything that you have experienced, felt, and kept bottled up for years without realizing it has and continues to affect you, your mind becomes clearer, and your communication with God clears and strengthens, allowing you to forgive others and hear God.

Look at your existence, all your accomplishments, and failures. Yes, you have made the wrong choices, decisions, and mistakes. Everyone, including you, and I are imperfect. No one person is better than the other or without fault. We fall, but we get back up. We are wounded, but we heal. We go through, but we come out on the other side. Forgiveness and the love of God can and will make you whole again when you fall, are harmed, and go through things.

The battle is not physical. It is spiritual and based on what is going on deep within you and what you are feeling. Communicate with yourself and God. Issues from your past not dealt with causes new issues, inner-guilt, projection of those situations on current situations, and keeps you from your destination in God's plan. Work on yourself so that decisions you make moving forward will not only build you up but also not cause further conflicts and impede your Godly journey and purpose. You must trust God to guide you while being okay with who you are and love yourself.

You have so much more to do during your journey. Being unforgiving and desiring revenge is not a viable choice and will ultimately lead you down the wrong path, away from God and fulfillment of your purpose (Colossians 3:12-17; Romans 12:17-19).

You must realize that what occurred cannot be undone. Where you go from here, how you proceed forward, and decision-making is essential to living your best life and fulfilling God's will and purpose for you. You most likely have major decisions to make about your future following God's will. You must be clearheaded and in a calm space to make the right decisions.

Also, remember someone is always watching you. First and foremost, God is watching. If you have children, they are watching. You are an example for them. All those closest to you are watching as well. We inspire each other through our love and actions. The thing a lot of individuals do not realize is that absolute strangers may also be watching and influenced by your behavior. Why does a stranger's opinion matter? You never know. Your behavior displays the type of person you are. If a stranger sees you exhibit forgiveness and love to someone who distressed you, they see the Godliness in you. It could ultimately draw them to God. Trusting God is the first step. When you trust in God, everything else will fall into place. No matter the situation, God will guide you through and elevate you (1 Peter 5:6-11).

I remember, on many occasions, losing it when I was hurt. I would call people derogatory names and talk to them or about them disrespectfully. I even desired to harm them because of the pain they caused me physically. Though it can occur in the form of mental, physical, or emotional pains, it feels physical and hurts like a substantial injury. I have been physically, mentally, and emotionally grieved. Nine times out of ten, I reacted in an unGodly, unforgiving manner at the time of occurrence. I was wrong to act that way. While it is easy to allow one's flesh (revenge-seeking) to lead over the spirit (love) is a normal occurrence in this imperfect world we live in (Galatians 5:19-26).

I incorporated praying and reading the bible while taking a discerning look at myself. I asked God to let me forgive myself and help me to see what HE sees in me. I prayed that God forgives me and that HE helps me forgive myself. I realized that I am not perfect and will make mistakes and that I had to get back up, repent, and keep moving forward to fulfill the purpose God has for me. It did not happen overnight. Eventually, I stopped blaming myself, realized I had made wrong choices, and knew that God had forgiven me. I learned to walk in the present and let go of the past. Most importantly, I did my best to learn from my mistakes and did my best to learn from them. (Psalm 139; John 3:16 and 8:32; Matthew 26:28; 1John 1:9; Romans 3:23 and 5:1, and 8:1; 2 Corinthians 5:17; Philippians 4:8).

Forgiving Others

After forgiving yourself, you must forgive all others concerned, meaning those involved internally and externally. Pray to God to help you with this. Pray for the people that grieved you. It may be hard to do at first, but it gets easier as you continue to do it. God will help you. After some time passes, it will get better, and you will slowly get back to the place you need to be to follow God and do HIS will while fulfilling your purpose.

Some people believe that the individuals that harmed them do not deserve to be forgiven and find it hard to do so. I sure did not want to forgive anyone. I soon learned that forgiveness is for our benefit, not for their benefit. Not forgiving gives a hold on you or control over you to the person that harmed you because you will not forgive them. Take control and forgive. Do it for God and yourself. Call on God for help. HE is always there with and for you. You must regain and be in control of yourself, your decisions, and your actions. You must be in control to willingly do things in accordance with God's will. Trust God! Know the best is yet to come, and you will be happy again, even if it does not feel like it right now.

Again, I prayed and read the bible, asking God for help. Times arose when topics came up, or memories surfaced, and I caught myself about to say something derogatory about the individuals that distressed me. However, I would stop ask God to forgive me and rephrase my statements and feelings. It takes work and determination. It can be accomplished. Believe in God and yourself as his child. (Psalm 55:22; Matthew 6:14, 22:34-40; Proverbs 16:4; Hebrews 12:14; Colossians 3:13; Ephesians 4:32).

Confidence

Forgiveness is not the only issue I had to handle. I realized that confidence played a big role in my healing, as well. Forgiving is essential, but to continue moving forward involves having confidence in the person God created you to be and the purpose you are to fulfill.

I watched my mother searching for validity and happiness in a man and not God my whole adolescence and teen years, until her death. If a man paid her attention and complimented her, she would be happy and bless everyone with her beautiful smile. She was a gorgeous woman, and everyone knew it except her. She did not need a man to validate and love her as much as she thought she did. So many people adored my mother. She had a loving personality and gave to anyone needing anything she possessed. I swore to myself growing up that I would never seek validation and happiness through a man.

Well, I guess there is no denying I am my mother's child. What did I do? I sought validity, confidence, and happiness from men, just like ma did. In the beginning, all it took was a smile and a compliment from a man. As time went by the same men that built my confidence, made me happy, and made me feel valid were doing and saying things to decrease my confidence and destroy me. The process it once took to increase my confidence, happiness, and validity had become more complex because of how easy it became for the men in my world to snatch it away.

I gained my confidence from the wrong sources, men. When men started to pay me attention and gave me compliments, I valued and welcomed it. It gave me such self-esteem and confidence that I could do whatever I set my mind to do. It made me feel beautiful and unstoppable. What I did not realize is that in most cases, the same way you gain something, you will lose it also.

The men I believed in and trusted impelled my confidence into depletion and a barren wasteland. Instead of gaining confidence from my Creator, God, the almighty, I gained it from imperfect men and their attempt to obtain something from me. God created you and me. God makes no mistakes. We are wonderfully and marvelously made in HIS image (Psalm 139:14). Is that not enough to instill confidence in oneself?

There is no person alive that is perfect and absent of flaws, whether inherited, due to injuries, or other reasons, except for Jesus. Each flaw is a display of who we are and the strength we have procured throughout the trials and tribulations of our lives.

I remember when I had my first neck surgery. It left a visible scar down the front left side of my neck. I never liked clothes that covered my neck because it was short. After the neck surgery, I decided to wear turtlenecks to cover up my scar. I was so uncomfortable and miserable the whole time I wore them. Ironically, my second husband told me not to hide it because it was a part of my story and battles that I had fought and won. I looked in the mirror and realized that scar displayed a battle I fought and won by the mercy and grace of God. Now I wear clothes I like and am comfortable in and wear that scar and all the others like the trophies they are. Each one of a person's scars and flaws displays that God's grace and mercy continually prevail, and HE has provided and taken care of us through the dark, scary, and painful times.

We will all go through things and come out with scars, bruises, and pains. We cannot let them define us. Allow God to define who you are and build up your confidence. If you do this, you will never lose it, and no one will be able to decrease or defile it (Psalm 139:13-16).

I learned to focus on what I was able to do, and not my difficulties and flaws. I learned to love myself and realize I am a child of God and deserve to be loved. If I focus on God, HE will send me the man HE created for me and all will work for the glory of God (Romans 8:28-30; Psalm 27:14, 123:1-2, and 145:15-16; 1 Corinthians 4:5; Hosea 12:6).

Forgiveness & Confidence Guides You Forward in God's Purpose & Plan

My aunty/mommy, children, best friend, and others close to me were spending all their time comforting me and trying to help me get through all my experiences. I absolutely love and appreciate each of them. They helped, but only when I finally gave all my pain and grief to God and forgave all involved did peace follow. It came slowly, but abundantly so I could get back on track and move forward. After some time, my peace returned and descended on my family members as well (Proverbs 3:1-2).

Although I was able to gain my peace and strengthen my relationship with God, I still lacked the confidence in myself I once had. The actions and words from the men I encountered had once again had me second-guessing myself and feeling worthless. After finding my peace and strengthening my relationship with God, I needed to work on myself and correctly rebuild my confidence and validity, according to God, not men. I started focusing on my relationship with God by studying HIS word, praying, fasting, and

trusting HIM more than I ever have. Immediately my world began to change for the better. True happiness comes from God and doing HIS will. God will forgive your inequities and forget them. HE will throw them in the sea of forgetfulness (Micah 7:19).

Forgive those who hurt you and free yourself while allowing God to build your confidence. Unlike man, God is perfect and never changes. HE will love and remain by your side forever. God's arms are always open to you even when mankind's are not. God will never leave or forsake you.

Once you forgive, let go and give it to God, and begin to focus on HIM. HE will give you all the confidence you require and begin blessing you right in front of those who wanted to bruise, harm, or even destroy you. Trust God in everything you do.

While I may not have 100% confidence in myself yet, (maybe 84%), it is growing, and I am still standing. I know I have a purpose, I am beautiful, and most importantly, I am a daughter of the KING.

The Butterfly Has Metamorphosized

In retrospect, as I wrote this chapter, I found myself asking, how did I do it and get to this frame of mind? I know you are also wondering. The best, most meaningful, and the only answer is God. Living is not an easy process. It took many years before I grasped the need for God and continuous transformations. Next comes forgiveness, which also is not easy. It is worth all the effort and work you must put into it, and I wish I had understood the significance of forgiveness and embraced it a lot sooner. I found the cure for each of my painful experiences. It is God, forgiveness, confidence, and loving God and yourself. God will make a way where there seems to be no way (Isaiah 43:19).

In each of these situations, once I embraced God, forgiveness was not far behind.

Pain, emotions, harm, and trauma, cause anger and hatred, which block love. Forgiveness removes anger and hurt, promoting love. Forgiveness not only heals; it makes room for love. I know you may be saying, I am crazy for even saying that, but it is so true. I felt the same way when an awesome friend and sister-in-Christ told me that I must find forgiveness in my heart. She explained that it is what God wanted me to do. No matter how many times we are injured, we must continually forgive (Matthew 18:21-22).

I have gone through my maltreatments, been harmed, felt guilty, and experienced many tribulations. I have had two divorces (2nd just finalized), many surgeries, relationships (some with closure and some without), and have overcome each of them with the help of God. I have learned forgiveness and practice it daily. When it is hard, I call on God for assistance. I am confident and still standing. I have transformed into the beautiful, confident butterfly God created me to be. Today I am confidently standing on the promises of God and not those of man. I know that there will be more trials and tribulations in the future. However, I also know God is with me and will make a way for me to fulfill the objectives I have in HIS ultimate plan.

Will I find true love? Will I marry again? I do not know the answers to these questions. As I was created to be a helper and compliment to the man God created for me, I do want a healthy and fairy tale inspired relationship. While I may not know the future or my outcome, God does, and I trust HIM. I know I am beautiful, have flaws and scars, and am imperfect. Those flaws and scars are mine and the trophies of my accomplishments and conquests. I have overcome, only because I placed my faith in God and not man. Give it to God, forgive, believe in yourself, trust God, embrace your change, and stand.

This butterfly (me) has emerged from her cocoon, trusting God, putting HIM first, and knowing who she is. She is embracing life and all that comes with it, open for love, walking in my destiny in God's plan, and still standing. You can do it too, just embrace your change and stand, relying on God (Proverbs 3:5-6).

Words of Wisdom

You more than likely loved the person that pained or harmed you. If you did not, it would not have discomforted you as bad. True love is Godly love and deep inside you. You still do have love for them, whether you want to or not. This was one of the hardest concepts for me to understand. Once, I truly gave it to God and forgave the men who hurt me; I realized that I yet had Godly love for them even though I was no longer in love with them or believed I required them. In all honesty, I did not want to love them still because it would be easier if I did not care.

The greatest lesson I have ever learned came through being hurt by those I loved the greatest. Even after being grieved to my core, once I forgave, I realized I yet loved the person who had hurt me the worst. I thought I was crazy. God's love made the lesson I was to learn clear. Love is a gift from God, and God is love. We fall short and pain God daily, yet, HE still loves us and does not give up on us. Imagine how many times our actions sadden and pain God, yet HE loves us the same yesterday, today, and tomorrow. Never allow pain and trauma to stop you from loving. This lesson freed me from many feelings that are not of God (1 John 4:7-21).

When hatred, a work of the flesh, prevails, we are not living in spirit and truth. When we forgive and allow God and love to prevail, we are. Let nothing and no one keep you from God and the ability to fulfill your purpose. Draw close to HIM and cast all your pains and fears upon HIM (Psalm 55:22).

Forgiveness and confidence are products of God's "agape" love. The devil does not want us to forgive others, have confidence, or to love in this way because it draws us closer to God. The devil seeks to destroy us and prove we are unworthy of God's love, yet God will provide a way out for HIS children (1 Peter 5:8-9). Yes, we must cope with the pain and hurt, but God will restore you in HIS time just as HE will destroy the devil (Revelation 20:10).

Just as there is a line between love and hate, there is a line between God and the devil. Which side do you want to be on? The devil does not want us to love. He wants us to live against all of God's principles. If the devil tempted Jesus, why would he not tempt us? Pain, heartache, and tribulations are situations and perfect scenarios for the devil to come in if you are not careful (Job 1:8-11).

There are good and bad aspects of all things. There is only one thing, the trinity, or persons of God, Jesus, and Holy Spirit that are all good. People are not all bad. Their human aspect, imperfection, and free choice allows people to make mistakes and wrong choices. There will be good times and bad times. God wants you to love HIM first and then yourself. If you cannot love yourself, how can you love someone else? You had your share of good and bad. Did the good outweigh the bad? If you say, "no" that was God's provisions and protection. If we seek God, submit to God, forgive, let go, let God, have faith in God, trust in God, love God, obey God, hope in God, love ourselves, love others, and walk in all of the glory God is, we will be found standing (Matthew 22:34-40). Do not let the devil use the bad to outweigh the good. Trust me; he will if you let him.

Vengeance belongs to God, not us. God will handle the situation; you just forgive (Romans 12:17-21). Forgive those who pained, harmed, or took part in your trials and tribulations negatively. Free yourself, put God first, love and forgive yourself, walk-in God's glory, and be the person HE created you to be. Show love, display Godliness, walking confidently in your destiny and place in God's plan. He will equip your every need and even your desires when you walk the path, HE chose for you (Isaiah 58:11).

Be the forgiving butterfly God created you to be. Embrace your metamorphosis and exit your cocoon, knowing God is with you. Walk confidently in your purpose, knowing God created you wonderfully and will supply your needs. You are the forgiving butterfly that is confident and walks in God's given purpose. Fly butterfly fly!!!

I pray each of you reading this chapter is blessed by something I have said or gone through, and it benefits and assists your healing and journey, then I am blessed.

Be Blessed

Gina

The following two affirmations are my gift to assist with your journey in becoming and being that butterfly God created you to be. Say the first one daily as you heal and begin to build your confidence. When you feel confident, read both daily and began your walk and Godly-filled, purposeful journey.

Affirmation #1

I am magnificently made by the great CREATOR, God
God makes no mistakes
I am not a mistake
While I am imperfect, I am who God created me to be
I have a purpose and God has a plan
I will be bruised, go through trials and tribulations, and struggle at times
My faith and trust in God will get me through
I will forgive those who harm and wound me, for myself and not them
I will love them whether near or far
I will pray for them as well
I will trust and confess my iniquities to God
In doing so, I ensure God forgives me and throws my iniquities into the sea
God knows my heart, and I know HIS love
I am a beautiful, amazing, child of the King, and amazingly made by HIM
I will embrace my scars, flaws, and imperfections
I will not allow them or anything to stop me from fulfilling my purpose in God's plan
Today and every day moving forward I will shine in all the glory God created me in
Amen! Amen! Amen!
By Gina Erwin

Affirmation #2

I have embraced my change and I am transformed
The preceding caterpillar is now a beautiful butterfly
Today and for the rest of my life I will spread my wings and fly high
My scars and flaws are mine and are part of my beauty
They display my overcoming & conquests with the assistance of
God
I am with God, and HE is with me
God fills my heart with HIS love and my soul with confidence
HE loves, holds, guides, and protects me in every moment
I am not exempt from suffering and will periodically experience it
Through it, all, God's love, grace, and mercy will prevail on my
behalf
I will walk with my head held high looking up to where my help
comes from
I will forgive others because God said so
I will be confident because God created and empowers me to be so
I will succeed because God is with me
I will be the butterfly God designed me to be with all my beautiful
markings
I am a beautiful, confident butterfly
No one has the power to take that away from me except God
Here I stand ready to fly
AMEN! AMEN! AMEN!
By Gina Erwin

Gwendolyn DiFernando

Gwendolyn is a single hands-on 'mompreneur' who owns and operates her boutique skincare salon. She is embellished with 12 years of experience as an owner/operator. She provides stellar knowledge and attention to her clients. Gwendolyn is a divorcee of seven years and has two children, a girl and a boy aged 12 and 14, who are the center of her life. Her greatest accomplishment is conceiving, birthing, and continuing to nurture her two children at age 40+.

She is an expert in esthetics, passionate to assist others in feeling their best, and is dedicated to her children and friends. Becoming an author regarding life as a divorced single mom is something that she has desired since her separation. She looks forward to reaching and touching others with words, guidance, empowerment, while inspiring women with her intricate journey after divorce. Gwendolyn now has an elevated reliance on God.

Favorite Scripture

1 Corinthians 13:4-13

Love is patient, love is kind. It does not envy, it does not boast, it is not proud. It does not dishonor others, it is not self-seeking, it is not easily angered, it keeps no record of wrongs. Love does not delight in evil but rejoices with the truth. It always protects, always trusts, always hopes, always perseveres. Love never fails. But where there are prophecies, they will cease; where there are tongues, they will be stilled; where there is knowledge, it will pass away. For we know in part and we prophesy in part, but when completeness comes, what is in part disappears. When I was a child, I talked like a child, I thought like a child, I reasoned like a child. When I became a man, I put the ways of childhood behind me. For now we see only a reflection as in a mirror; then we shall see face to face. Now I know in part; then I shall know fully, even as I am fully known. And now these three remain: faith, hope and love. But the greatest of these is love.

Dedication

First, I dedicate the purpose of this chapter to offer hope and confidence to women in similar predicaments. Secondly, I write to honor my mother and father for providing the foundation to get me this far in this story called life! My divorced parents, who have remained close friends for over 30 years, have invariably and unconditionally loved me and backed whatever aspirations I pursued. My parents accompanied us (along with my sister) in the delivery room with both of my babies, and they have held my family up in every segment of our lives. I do not express enough how much I appreciate and love them for the strength, patience, love, and care they give me and my children!

The Purple Flesh-Eating Fish

By: Gwendolyn DiFernando

As women, we get married with a hunger to commit ourselves to the person we love. We hope to create a lifetime of love and happiness. We desire to build a deep trust, friendship, and relationship with God together. Many of us marry with the grandiose dream to begin a family. We make a commitment hoping to live with a bond that will keep us strong by forming a united front and exist as a couple that grows in each other's love while serving God. Perhaps, the marriage erodes. We add expectations, disappointment, negative criticism, selfishness, and eventually, the boondoggle (intertwining rubber keychain) we made becomes unraveled. The rubber is bent, crooked, lax, and cannot stay together. In which case, we face divorce.

Life starts over again and resumes, differently. We are alone. However, we bring the companionship of our bruises, scars, fears, and pain to the next natural path of our life. Often, well, many times, no one can see our scars. We do not notice them until they suddenly bubble into our daily lives and most definitely into a new relationship. Slowly, but sometimes abruptly, we find ourselves reliving the daily pains of our broken marriage repeatedly and on many occasions, we struggle with it. If left untreated, it can resurface with our children or new love. Divorce scars can heal, or keloid and leave large unsightly bumps and pocks that are uncomfortable and often unpleasant to deal with. Scars can make us self-conscious and add to a lack of self-confidence. We need to carefully choose how to repair those scars. Sometimes we use an ointment that cannot get to the actual healing, but only helps superficially. This is my journey of divorce scars. My prayer is this allows your scars to heal faster and allow you to become whole.

Shortly after my separation, I discovered a term describing a cross between a narcissistic and sociopath personality. My personal term for narco-path is "The Purple Flesh-Eating Fish (PFEF)". This term is derived from a long-time close friend and observer. She described me as the pretty little purple fish who swims along seeking happiness while the mean big fish (narco-path) comes and attempts to eat me until I float on my side (at the top of the tank). *Capisce?* Many of the blended behaviors of this personality type are what I endured repeatedly throughout my marriage and divorce. Stay with me.

The Beginning

Marriage and children were my long-time desires. At 39, we tied the knot. I delivered my son at age 40. *Yes,* he was my honeymoon, baby! I *still* need to get the t-shirt that reads (*Made in Italy)* for my son. His birth was such a great blessing. I was goo-goo over him (still am). I could not think of having another child, due to my overflowing love for him.

When he was 11 months old, I felt an intuition. I woke up and thought, *"We need to have a baby for him. He needs a sibling!"*. Shazam, 11 months later, I gave birth to our baby girl! Ladies, we conceived our son on the first attempt and our daughter on our second try, at age 40 and 42, respectively. Truly, this was a gift from the grace of God.

Unraveling

While married, I did not realize my husband possessed (*no pun intended*) this narco-path personality disorder. Seven years ago, my ex-husband asked me to leave our home. Honestly, there was no valid reason. He and I were getting along on all levels. My skincare business was accelerating; our children were getting along *(not constantly, of course),* and I began to carve out time for exercise. It was what I described as a letter grade "*B*" marriage. I was developing a stronger version of me, and my new boosted independence made him uneasy. He felt he could no longer control me or my emotions. He grew increasingly uncomfortable as I became more confident in my own self-worth. It caused him to feel like he was losing control.

We attended marriage counseling, essentially, the *whole* marriage. I sporadically experienced physical and emotional anxiety. With the help of one of our marriage counselors, I finally realized that my anxiety was in the way of a clear mindset. It was situational, mentally brought on by my relationship, and physically due to the end of my adorned breastfeeding era.

After searching for several methods to combat my ever-changing estrogen, my primary care physician helped me find anti-anxiety medications. Consequently, it allowed me to see what was transpiring in my marriage and enabled me to be less desperate for my ex-husband's approval. The anxiety was not *all* his responsibility, although hands down, I was caught in the web of passive-aggressive approval. I often wonder how women handled this situation some 50+ years ago. How did they help themselves when they, too, experienced anxiety after pregnancy and/or breastfeeding? Something tells me perhaps an adult beverage helped their situation (*that is simply my take, just speculation).* At times, physical anxiety robbed me of the peace I deserved in my life. I was grateful I found a solution to help it subside.

My ex-husband asked me to leave our home. He wanted to end our marriage. I was confident in what I gave to our marriage. I had a full awareness that we could not live, grow, or nourish each other nor our family unit. It was a toxic environment for me and ultimately him. I was sure-footed; it was the right thing for myself and our children. After experiencing three marriage counselors, I became stronger emotionally, I was certain our marriage needed to be dissolved and was unhealthy. I took a huge leap, and I truly was not sure how it all would transpire. I knew I had to depart and start living as a single parent.

I did not fear the change, yet I had encouragement for a better life for my children, and hopefully someday a more suited healthy partner. I knew if I remained in that dynamic, I would get eaten by the Purple Flesh-Eating Fish. I had faith in God that I could make this huge move. There was a part of me that questioned my commitment to God and my marriage. I did not feel like we had any components of a Christian marriage. I knew I had exhausted all I could. Yet, admittedly, I probably could have prayed more.

He lost control over my emotions and wanted me out. When I agreed to leave the house, he did not realize I was taking our children with me. After all, I was their full time, *hands-on* mom (*at that time he worked six days a week. I am not sure why he thought our kids would not be with me?*). We faced divorce proceedings for three consecutive years prior to our split. The moment he realized I truly *was* leaving was the moment he snapped. He was no longer the same man I once knew. He completely lost his passive-aggressive stance and outward anger-filled our home for three months prior to our departure. There was so much hostility, plain untruths said to my children, and so many made-up stories, all with the intent for our children to mirror the anger he carried for me. My once calm, passive-aggressive ex turned (*snapped* is more appropriate). He had abruptly shifted into an outwardly angry man. I had not witnessed this side of him, ever, nor had the kids. When he lost control of me, anger erupted! *Hello, lava pouring down daily.* It was game on.

During our last three months of living *apart* in our home, it became volatile. I knew we were separating although I was unsure *how* I was going to make it happen. To spend as much time apart, I ventured on my own to the mountains with our young ones (*it was a big thing for me to drive there by myself-huge*). My son begged me to go to a lonely diner that we passed (*I am simply not a diner kind of girl*). While lunching, a gentleman (*stranger*) and his son made small talk about boy scouts. We were the only patrons in the place, by the way.

Upon our arrival back home, I could feel the tension in the air. I knew my ex was *surprised* I drove solo plus two (our kids). Shortly after I put our children to bed, my ex-husband literally snatched our children out of their beds and fled with them to our master bedroom. He locked me out and interrogated our children. I was upset at the fact that he disturbed their sleep. I was infuriated he locked me out of our bedroom. I stayed calm. *I am not sure how I did.* The culmination here is, my ex asked, *"Did mommy meet any men in the mountains?".* They said, *"Yes, some guy named Nick".* Their innocent answer was real. We did have a brief conversation with a man named Nick and his son at the diner. My ex-husband exploded in front of our kids, accusing, *"You planted a man in the mountains, and you wanted the kids to think you just met him!"* (Am I really writing this?). The crazy got crazier. He was convinced I was leaving the marriage due to the man in the mountains.

Yes, Ladies, *I cannot make this up*. This was pure character assassination. Could I have been leaving because of his behavior throughout our marriage or the way we interacted with each other? How about the fact that he kicked me out of our home?

Continuing this pseudo comical (terrible for our children) story, the ex-husband intruded into my Facebook account. He required our children to identify "Nick" from the mountains. Yes, he sat them at our computer and made them identify the accused cheatee! Under the crazy pressure, they picked out one of my client's husband (same name-Nick). He then spent *years* trying to convince them and my family that I had a boyfriend and was a cheater. There was no validity to this accusation, just unhealthy behavior for our children from someone who lost his passive-aggressive control.

He was angry and disgruntled as I packed up the house each week. I remember he took a huge knife and started opening the boxes, angrily, yet calmly, with our children watching. He removed items out of the boxes one by one. A few times during the three months before I could physically depart, I had to call the police for help. On random mornings, he would again grab our children and whisk them to his car. He would exclaim, *"C'mon kids, daddy's taking you to work. You don't have to stay here with her!"*. Our innocent children thought it was exciting. They were going to work with daddy! Yet, they felt the enormous conflict, almost forcing them to choose which parent they were going to heed. On two occasions, maybe three, I stood behind the car and calmly stated, *"I don't think so"*, while I made my non-emergency call to the police. The policeman arrived and told him, *"Go to work where you belong and mom, take these kids in the house where they belong!"*. *Word*.

It was so painful listening to him derive lies and bad-mouth me to our children, *so painful*. I was fearful of the effect of the accusations my children were absorbing. I could not bear for their little souls to hear such horrible lies about me. Looking back, it pains me to relive the drama our little children endured. They did not realize they were being used as weapons. This also planted the seed that mommy was bad, and daddy was good.

Another time, he was verbally bashing me to our children, I called 911. I was uncertain of him snapping and was afraid. Are you ready? He picked up the other landline. *(Yes, Ladies, we had landlines)*. He began telling the 911 operator what a terrible person I was and that I was cheating with a guy I claimed I met in the mountains. I wish I could say I was joking about this. I exclaimed, *"This is **my** 911 call. You do not get to hijack my 911 call! Get off my call!"*. Can you imagine what the operator was thinking? I am quite sure that we were someone's comedic relief in a conversation somewhere passed along.

Are you ready for this Ladies? As I prepared for a new life *sans* (without) husband, there were many projects to check off. I had two small children; my urgent task was to find a new school in less than three weeks. I chose their school based on my imploring clients, friends, and teachers for recommendations. I was on the hunt. I found an amazing elementary school with many accolades. The PFEF was not having any part of it. Flash to me pacing up and down the streets of our city's downtown, on the exterior of my lawyer's office. It was 6:30 PM on the Friday prior to the first day of school. Mamma was on a mission for her son's first-grade attendance at his new school, and to have my little one stay put for her upcoming transitional kindergarten class. The PFEF was on a mission for them to attend the same school near our former home. I, along with her outstanding teachers, recommended transitional kindergarten. *I do not understand the urgency to have any of our children rush through such a nourishing time of their youth and education.* Her teachers and I agreed kindergarten would be a huge step at such a young age, while she was coping with the divorce. I literally walked up and down the streets for an hour waiting for our two lawyers to contend our stances for the best choice for our two little children, ages five and seven, (I have two words, sickening and ignorant). *Literally, in October 2019, seven years later, my ex-husband dropped a text and thanked me for the decision I fought him for regarding our daughter's education.*

Do Not Engage

Let us move forward with "How *not* to engage with a narco-path". I will now explain what happened to me when I *engaged* the narcopathic PFEF. There are many severe acts my ex-husband quietly performed. I say *quietly* because he attacked, while no one was watching. The attacks were relentless. It resembled a silent war that I wanted no part of. However, it **was** war. Immediately, during the separation in our home, he was extremely angry because he lost control of my mind and my soul. During the marriage, he quietly played with my soul and my mind like a puppeteer. My emotions were a string he chose to pull and manipulate. He withdrew affection like a power tool. It is a trait.

My children and I faced extreme behavior from the PFEF upon our departure from our home. This continued for seven years. His extreme behavior mirrored another trait of a narco-path/narcissist. I was not aware I married this personality. I was tricked into an unhealthy state of mind of what is *"normal"*. Immediately after we separated, I worked hard to fight the horrible energy in our home for three months. I tried to keep our children protected from the tension; still, I was defeated. There was no way to shelter our children from it.

Single Mom

We packed up. *I think I rented a truck.* Today, I cannot remember how we transferred everything from one home to another. In our case, straight out of our three-bedroom ranch home, I landed a two-bedroom apartment. It was a very pleasant, good looking apartment with upgrades that appeared more like home. I set my children up in the master bedroom. Here, I created two bedrooms within the large master layout. I graciously chose the smaller bedroom. I was never quite ready for the next elements I faced. Bedtime was an innate part of who I was when they were young. Now, I was not with my children every night. I could not always tuck them in. I did not get to kiss them goodnight regularly. It was a huge, huge transition. Although I thought the divorce process through, I was simply not quite ready for the impact of reality. Initially, it did not feel good. In fact, it felt so empty and plain wrong. I repeat, it just felt wrong!

Nick from the mountains became a sore/ridiculous spot in our new home. My son, then age seven, seemed to enjoy getting a rise out of his dad. This would make me steam. His dad worked six days a week, with long hours during our marriage. He was starving for his dad's attention. This *"Nick"* taunting allowed our son a venue to have more engagement with his dad.

There was a tiny part of me, at times, that was able to exhale. When my ex-husband occupied his legal custodial overnights, there was a delicate portion of my inner being that was able to breathe. A part of me was able to ponder my life, digest my thoughts of my changing reality, and grasp an opportunity to recharge and prepare for our children to return home. I am quite sure I never got to a full battery because there was so much transformation occurring.

Mommy Guilt

Mommy guilt has strength. It is like a tornado that sweeps in on a beautiful sunny day. I could be amid accomplishing great things and great achievements for my children, and suddenly there is a storm in my head about what I forgot. Was I kind enough? Did I yell too much? Should I have made dinner? Mommy guilt sometimes hit me like a snowball on the side of the head. I think we all know what that feels like, most likely. Truly, truly, truly, it serves no purpose in my life. It did not help me prosper as a parent. It did not help me become the mom I strived to be. It stopped me in my tracks and has, at times, stopped my 220-volt on a 110-volt energy. While enmeshed in mommy guilt, it impeded what could have benefited my children and me.

Mommy awareness is quite different than mommy guilt. As a single, divorced mom of two, I desired to give my children all I could. I sacrificed my own well-being. If I allowed it, I could have wallowed in mommy guilt every single day regarding a place where I fell short somewhere in my parenting process. I just do not see how possibly my mommy guilt nurtured my soul or our family unit. Somehow, through counseling, prayer, books, and programs, I knew mommy guilt was something that I needed to conquer. There is just no room at the inn for it! Mommy guilt robbed me of pure joy. It robbed me of the accomplishments I made. It sucked me into an emotional hole. Consequently, I could not be all that I desired to be for our children when I was debilitated emotionally. Mommy guilt is like a flat tire. It happens among us. It slows our momentum. It stops our progress and creates a slow roll.

I found myself constantly preparing their bedrooms. This task became therapy for me. I spent my weekends folding their clothes, making outfits, cleaning their rooms, and organizing their drawers. I tried to create a cozy, snuggly environment to my best effort. I sought out the resemblance of a comfortable, safe home in our new quarters. In fact, seven years later, I am still enduring this task for my *not* so little ones.

Ultimately, over time, the set-up became a disaster. Bedtime was a "Ringling Brothers Circus" episode. My then five-year-old daughter needed to fall asleep next to me. Consequently, they continuously fought over me and my attention. I slept with both taking turns. He, my then seven-year-old, wiggled, poked, pestered, and bounced. He *was* Tigger. This was not a fun bedtime scene. My little guy hassled, joked, and jumped on us. I could go on. Bedtime (aka crazy time) morphed into a two-and-a-half-hour ordeal every single night for about five and a half years. I solicited help from girlfriends, siblings, and my parents. I solicited advice from counselors. I cannot tell you the amount of help that I sought after. Nonetheless, I was never able to control the rambunctious nighttime energy in our new, single-parent apartment home. Looking back and reanalyzing the scene, I should have managed the boundaries more effectively. Let me explain. I was a newly single mom, and I did not have a strong desire to play the *ultimate strict* parent. I did desire more order and less chaos. Unfortunately, our dynamics prevented it.

When I reunited with my children following their time with their dad, my greatest desire was nurture, nurture, nurture. Particularly, for me, the problem was I could not get a hold of the concept of *"who is the parent and who is the child?"*. At times, they would exclaim, *"It's Dad's Day"*. I remember I used to ponder and reply, *"No, this is wrong. I am your Mom EVERYDAY!"*. True story, hard to admit. I was up against their tough questions infused by the

PFEF. His thoughts, peppered with his negative sentiment regarding my being, were shoveled into their minds. It still happens to this day. I felt I had to explain myself continually because, in *their* minds, I was doing something wrong. The element did not matter. He attempted to convince our children something as little as me going to the laundromat was a wrong doing. It was a long, difficult road. What has changed is their age, maturity, and how I handle my reactions.

Not so surprisingly, my little guy took the alpha role. He was empowered by another adult (his dad). I worked hard to prevent that, and many times lost the battle. Hands-down, my oldest little one was the man of the house. On the flip side, I was so fortunate in other avenues. God love him; he is quite a smart kid. He helped me with everything. He is my human navigation system. He shopped with me, fixed anything, completed chores like a champion, and was our electronic wizard. My son was my go-to helper. I remember he found our lost hamster and meticulously removed the grill off the back of our refrigerator to rescue him. Today, he is still a rock star regarding his chores. He is very responsible. He does not realize how important this will be in college and adult life. My son took on a lot of responsibility as a young child. Part of it was his natural personality trait. He welcomed the leader role, it was that simple, and I know it is a blessing.

We all have outgoing personalities, and mine especially is filled with a great deal of energy. There was not a dull moment in our new home. We did not watch television. In fact, we did not own one until three years post moving in. Ironically, that same TV fell off my son's dresser last week during a sleepover. He and his two friends slowly came down the stairs with shrugged shoulders, hesitantly announcing, *"Mom, you are going to be mad"*. The television is now recyclable. All I can think of is *"Toy Story 3"* with the big garbage incinerator. Bye-bye TV. Did I mention he was jumping on the bed? Enough said.

I had a STRONG-WILLED little boy, who grew up rather quickly as he adapted to our new scene. He did not want his family to split; neither did my girl. My daughter wanted her momma, that is for sure. Looking back, I think I expected too much out of them. My responsibility was to find this gentle mix of discipline and empathy, knowing they might not understand any of this divorce drama. *I thought they did.* Not a proud moment right now. I understand they are children, and they are unfamiliar with how to process all the mayhem. There was so much mayhem. In my role as single mom, I thought I was making a strong structured environment, and I considered myself strict. I examined my actions and evaluated myself constantly. I did my best to parent as a separated mom who was new to the scene. I had a purple force against me undermining any rule I put in place. I remember getting frustrated with our family counselor when he explained we had a triangle of power in our home. I would exclaim to him, *"You come over and do it! I am doing all I can! You try it".*

Somehow, I needed to strike a balance between conveying right and wrong, along with setting and implementing boundaries. It is called ***parenting. One of us had to parent.*** My situation turned unmanageable since I was the only parent with rules. My challenge was and *is still* to parent while simultaneously not putting their father down because of the choices he makes. I had to parent and discipline our children while they parroted and mimicked his harmful rhetoric (still periodically happening). I intended to help our situation by pointing out what is unacceptable. When I attached discipline to their dad in any way, it sabotaged my own efforts. I tried to parent with my know-how and style. It was difficult and disruptive when their dad supported any of their disrespectful behavior. I kept guiding our children with God's words, thoughts, and values while keeping a moral compass of right and wrong. I preached and taught the golden rule. Regretfully and sadly, I cannot say that I followed that protocol thoroughly. I am sure that I unnecessarily added stress and anxiety to my sweet children's hearts when they had *nothing* to do with this divorce. My children (and *most children*) want their mom and dad to stay together. They are half mom, half dad. They really do not want to be caught in the crossfire. Although I had the greatest intentions, I outwardly critiqued their dad, comparing his thoughts and value system to mine. My reactive responses created additional strife and conflict in our lives. Many times, I vented to others *(How could I not?)* in earshot of our children. It is the same emotional harm. I am not super proud of exposing this. It is a tough thing to admit.

I had a multitude of tasks as a skincare business owner/operator flying solo. The perpetual list is too long to mention. I faced tricky situations when I was in Esthetician mode. I would receive the random call that my little one was sick. Work stopped abruptly with clients on my books. Someone had vomited or had an injury, and this mom was en route to the elementary school. At times, Mister Snow Miser tipped his hat and *poof*, we did not have power, and school was out of session. Again, this mom was on her way to the elementary school. These interruptions all occurred while I was required to have a smile on my face at my salon. Oh, and let us be clear, I failed because I did not always have a huge smile on my face. If I could rewrite the story, I would learn to master a magnificent poker face. It is my responsibility to put that library book on the shelf when I am in 9-to-5 mode (*I mean 9-to-9 mode).* I am *certain, it* was an epic fail for me (Sigh). In my practice, I must offer my clientele my *all,* while maintaining the business upkeep, a*nd take care of my two-little people.*

Here we were, my children attended two different schools, in a completely different home, and welcoming apartment living on the second floor. Should I talk about noise, now? We made noise. I drove both siblings to school, picked each one up every day, drove my son to soccer, and my daughter to tumbling. I volunteered once a month in their classes to facilitate a little lesson on healthy nutrition. I might have missed, perhaps, one field trip, each, since the commencement of preschool. Hence, I became Ms. Chaperone for both my bambinos. I was completely present in their lives while operating my growing skincare empire.

Swiftly, the full effect hit me, that I was single. I found myself alone, introduced to newfound freedom. Not *exactly* freedom, when I was consistently being harassed. Nonetheless, it was a new type of freedom (*and torture*). Sorry to report, it was a new state of being, coupled with the reality of not being with my children. I was literally both happy and sad all the time. I am grateful when my children spend time with their dad. I know that they are happy and having fun. Although I struggle with what he teaches them during their time together. Displaying *any* respect for me is not on the menu! I struggled with their unhealthy sleeping and eating habits after their custodial time with their dad. The consequence of poor habits equals sick children. Rules were non-existent at daddy's house. I divorced what became a Disney dad.

The PFEF spent a lot of his time swaying our children's brains about the terrible and destructive "Cruella" mom, he thought (believed) I was. Glancing backward at the past seven emotional years, I would change the instances of the hate displayed. Whereas, I know clearly, I could not change his behavior, I could have changed my reaction. I did not always have the strength that I have now. I operated in fear when I was attacked. Some days, I kept my composure, and some I did not. At times, my reaction revealed the war inside of my heart. I was literally in a war to protect myself and our children. He brought all the guns daily. I would text or call and reiterate their bedtimes, food choices, phone usage, showers; *you get where I am going here*. This backfired on me because when someone loses control over you and you offer them suggestions, you literally give them weapons against you.

In a healthy situation, a divorced dad would cooperate with you, keep you informed about your children's on-goings, and keep his anger and frustration on a platform far away from them. So, here is the *truth*. When I responded to my ex, and I knew he was in a steady volatile state of mind, I realized it was me, as well, causing harm for our children. That is a tough truth to realize. It is a task that takes patience and a plan. A close, special someone kindly pointed out that *I* was and had been contributing to the harm. When tangled in the verbal web, it is easy to respond. One response leads to another. I learned to have a plan of action. I have three responses; **"Thank you", "I understand", and "I will get back to you"**. It saved me many wrinkles. It is difficult to realize and face the harm I, too, created.

We have different parenting philosophies. His parenting style is simply, *"It is their choice"*. His thought process is *"I respect their decisions; I am not emotional about it"*. Whoopee, what a way to parent a five and seven-year-old. *I am glad you are not emotional about it (help me!).*

Promptly, following our separation of homes, he stockpiled their refrigerator with cases of soda. He is aware I aspire for healthy eating choices for my family. I prefer we eat as much of a clean, organic diet as possible. He also brought televisions into their bedrooms, **literally** the day I left. This resulted in confusing our children. Of course, for children, it is more fun to have soda at your fingertips and watch television at your leisure. *Did I mention they were five and seven-years young, with no dental insurance?* He eliminated rules in their home. This deliberate conflict in parenting styles ultimately pained our children. The bipolar rule setting of both homes, interrupted their bedtimes, sleep patterns, healthy lifestyles, and their perceptions of good-parent/bad-parent. Consequently, *I* endured the disruption of sick days and doctor visits. If our children were sick at school, it was this momma jumping through hoops to rescue them. That is just what I do, jump through hoops. At times, it was a difficult task to keep them healthy. Because I have an emphasis on a healthy lifestyle, he equates this to control. He led our children to believe that I was **controlling** them with healthy meal choices, further disrupting my discipline. *We had sugar and spice **every** day.* My motto is, let's not have sugar at *every* meal. Pace yourselves, people!

Parental Alienation Syndrome

Let us investigate Parental Alienation Syndrome (PAS). PAS is rampant among divorced families and hardly receives the press it deserves. I certainly know this from my personal experience and others traveling the journey of divorce. There is an abundance of tension, animosity, anger, greed, and retaliation. My children became the victims of our newfound divorce war. Perhaps the war was *not* so new. I learned in a study I read; it is primarily women who are the cause of PAS. Well, let me tell you something, my firsthand experience is, the *Father* holds the vengeance. *LET US KEEP GOING.*

My son's mind was my ex's weapon to hurt me. He could no longer emotionally reach me with any of *his* conceptions about me. My son primarily became the tool he used. I remember distinctly exclaiming to my ex, *"You cannot hurt me anymore; I simply do not care what you think".* My son was not aware of what was transpiring. Consequently, his disposition with me emulated his dad's negative false beliefs. Nevertheless, we remained intricately connected in our school and sports environments. We had our challenges from his *dad-infused* power. In her younger years, my ex-husband was unable to mentally reach our daughter with his PFEF views. She *was into* her momma. At that time, we were fastened like velcro to each other. I found myself answering these questions from my *then* seven-year-old son:

Where were you?

Who was here last night?

How much wine did you drink?

Were you out drinking?

You were not really at the gym, were you?

How much money did you spend on your purse?

You are spending our child support money on a purse for yourself.

While these statements and questions were invalid and inappropriate for a child to ask their mother, I knew my son was being programmed by the PFEF. I did not introduce any male interests to my children, and my ex-husband knew I barely drank alcohol.

Our son was the tough one. For him, nighttime was a festival of pestering me and my girl. That was the hand I was dealt. He stirred the pot, and he was energetically wound on (*dang you sugar*). Together, my children and I survived attempted PAS in many different circumstances and on several levels. It is a difficult emotional environment to live in. I continue to love my children through the struggle. His objective was to turn our children against me. Sadly, and presently, I am experiencing the same harmful dynamics with my daughter as I did with my son in the past. I believe they have flipped roles, and it is now my daughter who emulates the PFEF. It is emotionally draining for all. More importantly, PAS is real. I knew I was up against it. I witnessed it years prior in other extended family dynamics. I knew it was a possibility to lose my children's love due to brainwashing. It was and is very scary. I continually work to combat to avoid the pitfalls of PAS.

I was fortunate to find a wonderful counselor from an organization that charged on a sliding scale. We visited her weekly in our first year of separation. I believed it benefited our children. However, the PFEF did not support their counseling, and harmfully demeaned the counselor's role. This caused our children to protest attending, especially because they felt backed up by their dad. I am grateful for her care and kindness. I will never, ever, ever, ever forget what she said to me, ***"Destroy and conquer at all cost"***. She trembled when she revealed it to me. That was solely her statement to me after meeting with my ex-husband. I was not surprised; I was already living it.

Throughout single-mom hood, I frequently missed the 7 pm to 9 pm window of required phone calls to their dad. He continually threatened to file contempt of court charges. He demanded we exchange our children in a grocery store parking lot. This conveyed a message that their home was unsafe. When I arrived one minute late, he continued to threaten more contempt of court charges. Also, this planted the message that I was unworthy of his presence. By refusing to step a foot in our new home, or drive *near* our house, he exemplified extreme disrespect as this added to the attempted alienation. In fact, it was part of his recipe. His eccentric behavior made it difficult to gain my children's respect. I cannot express how many hundreds of emails and texts I have received from him threatening to file contempt charges against me. In many instances (almost all), he shared his anger and intent with our children. Imagine how they and other children felt when someone puts this stress and tension on young minds. They just wanted to go to school or have a fun day. Sadly, they were enmeshed in the psychotic, controlling, angry behavior of their dad causing fear in their mom. (Yeah. Fun).

The PFEF fought hard in our custody negotiations, which wasted precious time and a galore of money. He demanded a segment in our custody order requiring me to stay away from all sporting events on his legal custodial time until our children were 18 years of age. *HELLO PAS*. I was/am the hands-on mom who provided our children the engine of finding the sports leagues, signing them up, (keep those birth certificates handy) and mommy Ubering them to and from, three to four times a week. Now, some PFEF in a psychotic state of mind is going to tell me I cannot attend my children's sporting events on his custodial weekends; until they are 18? Where do you think I stood on that? I remember my lawyer, with whom I felt safe and protected, told me to just sign the order, and you will get full custody. He said, *"I'm sure his anger will subside"*. I respectfully and emphatically denied any such rule and was ready to fight in court. I had **NO IDEA** where I was going to muster up the legal fees. I was certain, beyond a doubt, I would be fighting in court. It turned out, minutes before the court battle, my ex conceded to the agreement I proposed. However, he demanded I refrain from attending their sporting events for *six months*. This, consequently, added to fighting for my children's respect and proper behavior.

Are you ready? I headed to the ex's house on our first Christmas Eve separated. I called the police and requested assistance as it was my legal day for custody. I predicted it might be an episode. I was holding a temporary agreement. They explained they could not assist me due to the order not being signed by a judge. They were empathetic and asked me to call again if I did not feel safe. He and

I had a written agreement. However, he would not allow our children to leave the house. Rehashing it makes me ill. Consequently, when he opened the door while declining me my legal custody, I stuck my foot in the door. I was annoyed at the least. I simply wanted to pick up our children and leave. I am almost certain it was the following Christmas day that I received a letter to appear in court. I was charged with criminal B&E. That is a term for criminal breaking and entering for anyone that is unfamiliar. Yes, I was charged on Christmas Day. To this day, I wonder if I should have let them stay and not lived through the chaos. I would have shielded them and avoided days away from my career preparing for a criminal trial. I remember standing before the judge, thinking, *"I have full custody of our children, and he is trying to put me in jail, really?"*. I was not afraid of jail. I was worried about who would take care of our children. I had a friend offer me the $1500 lawyer fee. It was difficult to accept. She proclaimed, "I will not let you go into that courtroom alone". We still tear up about it today. Her kindness meant so much to me. It took so much fear away that I could face the charges with representation. I was found innocent, and I repaid her the money over time.

Next, he called the Department of Social Services (DSS). He claimed I was dangerous to my son. Meanwhile, I have full custody. I am at their schools every month, take care of all their health concerns, am their full-time mom in my entrepreneurial world, and I have a DSS claim against me? I stayed calm, super calm. It truly never affected me. I met with the social worker two times over a period of seven months before the charges were dismissed. Yes, they kept the claim against me for seven months. I never let it affect me. It did not change my days. I am confident in the mother I am. I know how much I love my kids. I never entertained a discussion with the PFEF regarding the charge. I just let his hatred spew.

After years of exchanging texts and pointing out the cruel behavior he was exhibiting to our children, he had me arrested for criminal cyberstalking. I remember distinctly; I wrote an email with bulleted points listing all he said to our children and how detrimental it was to them. That was the email he did not like, *apparently*. The law states if you have three or more qualifying text, you can make the alleged criminal charge for cyberstalking. Yes, ladies, (*for real*), I had to borrow money again from friends ($1500) and retain a lawyer to fight yet another charge. There was no regard that *I* had hundreds and hundreds of harassing texts/emails from him. It is his right to submit that charge. I recall my lawyer arranged it so I would not have to occupy a jail cell. However, I marched downtown to surrender, get fingerprinted, mouth swabbed, and photographed.

I recall everybody looking at me so kindly. I remember it so distinctively. The magistrates and police officers all gently smiled at me. The officer who photographed conversed with me about what preschool his kids should attend. One officer apologized for having to perform the fingerprinting. He explained it was an unfair law. I did not let it affect me and I was never frightened. I was annoyed that I could not be at work, making a living for my children. That was the most difficult part. I had to borrow money to keep myself out of jail when my desire was to be working and earning money for my family. I questioned, *"Can I smile for the picture?" (hee-hee)*.

A few months later, he charged me with *misdemeanor cyberstalking*. I was not arrested due to the misdemeanor level. I remember it was my 50th birthday, and two female police officers entered my salon. I looked at my long-time best friend and said,

"Oh, no, this is going to ruin our night". I quietly asked, *"Are you arresting me because I have a big gathering tonight?"*. They did not arrest me. Both kind policewomen ended up back in my salon while off duty and became my clients. True story! I was so happy to take care of them.

There are more forces he has reckoned with that I cannot bring myself to write about. I will save them for another book. I unjustly owed the PFEF a minimal sum of money, just at $1000. He filed a contempt of court, and there I was, not working and back in court. He obtained a lawyer. I was pro-se (represented myself). This one was easy, or so I thought. His lawyer started the case off with, *"Your Honor, we seek jail time".* Within seconds, I was numb, blank, and shut down. It was odd for my persona to respond in that manner. I was not prepared for their request. I entered the room solo, and I was confident in my case (*I still do not care for his lawyer*). To be transparent, this came after years of my parents carrying us financially while he was unemployed, with not a cent to his name. The judge was super kind and helped me through as the PFEF was spewing lies. I remember stating, *"Your Honor, are we going down that road? Because if we are, I have a lot to say".* He stated, *"No, no, no, you are doing a great job staying on point".* I remember his giggle when he saw my feistiness surface. The judge ordered me jail time. However, he gave me six months to pay back the $1000 and ordered me to pay my ex's $500.00 court fees. So, the lawyer got a new sparkly bracelet, and my children were in lack of their needs. *Sickening.*

It was my responsibility to protect my children from the alienation, simultaneously, while I was being verbally attacked. He remained on his mission to convince my children how awful I am. It is my job to continue to be loving to our children and ignore them when they parrot him. After years of frustration, pain, and fear, I eventually learned to block his responses. I blocked his telephone calls and emails. It is rather simple to do, yet I did not have the courage in earlier years. This brought relief to my psyche. I conditioned myself to become immune to his thoughts. I learned, the quicker I did, the quicker I protected myself and my children from further emotional harm. There are times I must unblock for necessary communication about our children. Sometimes, even seven and a half years later, I fall weak. In fact, I did it today. I have learned to lean on God to help me get stronger through each attempt. I realize I cannot be hard on myself when I fall backwards. I now know my failure is my feedback. With each occurrence, I become stronger and wiser.

I had to calculate how to make my rent, care for my children full-time, be present at my salon and school, commute to and from school daily (sometimes two different schools), and have an on-time performance in court to fight the perpetual criminal charges. I had to sustain revenue and remain on point for my clients and constantly borrow funds for criminal court cases. My job was to complete all these tasks while hiding the circumstances, emotional stresses, and reality from our children. My children would recite, *"Mom, we know you are going to court today"*. I answered, *"No, I have to meet my accountant to sign papers for the business"*. Imagine, I scurried our children to school with lunches made, clothes prepared, homework complete, teeth brushed, and breakfast (*sometimes)* made. I was no stranger to the sign-in/tardy slip. I had that to-do list fulfilled while he, (the almost Disney dad), was sitting calmly in court, ready to attack and put their mom in jail. As my brother would say, "Nice". My stomach turns as I write this. Looking back, I *thought* I was not engaging. I *was,* and more damage occurred because of it. Translation was a tough, long bumpy road to earn respect from my children due to the exposure of hate they were faced with. It can be difficult at times to get respect from two parents armed with a united front. I bet it is much more obtainable than my path.

I tried to execute by being firm and stern with clarity. However, my close friends thought I was too tolerable of some of my children's behaviors. I did have a list of rules, you know, a visual. I am not sure that it lasted a week. I remember each year we had a thankful tree on our wall. We made it out of construction paper. We wrote on the leaves, the things we were thankful for. As they grew, we lost that tradition. Two years ago, when behaviors were elevated, I elected to make the tree on my own. I took a big poster board and drew a tree with leaves. On each of the leaves, I wrote out the utilities and how much they were. I followed with rent, sports cost, and food. *I said, "Here you are, guys, take a look-see at our thankful tree"*. I thought that was a good visual (sigh). My sis LOVED it and got a big kick out of it.

The PFEF strikes the hardest when he is alone. Throughout their growing years, to fight the attempted PAS, I made sure to inform friends, family, teachers, sitters, and primarily all who love and interact with our children about our delicate scenario and how our children were being swayed. It helped my children with a plethora of confusing thoughts and helped keep the bully off the playground. I needed an army of friends and family giving my children support and comfort to love BOTH parents. My sister tried diligently to show respect to each of us in front of the children. While I feel he did not deserve her respect, she did so for love of our children.

I attempted to keep the defense of myself to the barest minimum. The idea is to *not* defend yourself. I divorced a narco-path. I was continually blamed for everything and anything that occurred. Pick a topic; I was blamed. The important factor I learned, beyond a shadow of a doubt, was not to defend myself. No matter the accusation, no matter the lie, as soon as I defended myself, disruption occurred. It disrupted my personal growth, my accomplishments, career, mood, energy, and inner peace. My ex would recite past instances that occurred in our marriage. It seemed he had an ongoing battle in his mind, determined to convince himself what a horrific wife and mother I was. He used me and our children to convince himself. If I defended myself, I would have become his whipping post. It hurts to be whipped. A sentiment I carried around with me daily was, "*Why does he get to do this? Why does he get to act this way with no repercussion?*". No matter how hurtful or how influential he was to our children, he was held accountable and responsible to no one. This infuriated me. He was estranged from his family, and ultimately mine. He had minimal close friends. He had the freedom to verbally abuse. A favorite line I preached over and over was, "*Just because the abuse comes from his mouth does not mean you cannot feel the bruises*". I used to explain to my closest girlfriend, "*If you could see bruises from verbal abuse, my body would be black and blue*". She completely understood from her similar personal experiences. We lift each other up with love and encouragement to overcome the abuse. She is paramount in supporting my children and me.

The PFEF was on a mission to destroy my soul, and I was letting him. Although I am a strong, type A personality, outgoing, deliberate, with a huge supporting female tribe (a group of friends and family that support each other), I allowed him to take my happiness and peace away from our one-parent family unit. Summation, *I KNEW BETTER*. I knew my job was to ignore him, and I did regarding many circumstances. Ultimately, there are many instances I failed. My son parroted my ex's sentiment. It came out with all sorts of phrases. This is where I failed to lead with perseverance.

It was so difficult to hear my young son repeat my ex's mindset. *"Daddy says you spend his money on yourself. Daddy says you do not really work. Daddy says you do not care about us when you go to the gym. Daddy says, you are fake. Daddy says you go to our school just to 'look' like a good mom. Daddy says your birthday parties are a dog and pony show, so you look good. Daddy says, you are a freak. Daddy says, you lie".* Need I go on? I could fill a book (hee-hee). What made it more difficult was that he dropped the "*daddy says*" and continued to voice his dad's point of view. It was the HARDEST PART of the divorce for me. Again, I understood why my son was acting this way. Sadly, at other times, I handled it with too much emotion. I knew my children were upset due to our divorce. I recall telling them that they would get to see their dad a lot more because of our separation. I always held in my mind that my children did not want their parents to separate, period. They love us both.

Dating

When I started my new life journey, my first and foremost priority was my children. Naturally, I explored the idea of dating. At that time, I felt unleashed by someone constantly telling me I was wrong. In every aspect, cooking, thinking, working, cleaning, I was told I was doing it wrong. I was wrong because I wanted a lightweight stroller to tote around two toddlers, *(I was 43).* Yes, ladies, I was in trouble because I wanted/needed a stroller at age 43. *I bought the stroller.*

I am not certain why I started to date so quickly. I think a part of it was I had the freedom not to care. I had the freedom to be myself without ridicule. I did not want to EVER marry again. I carried that sentiment for years. I started exercising four years after my girl was born. I was feeling energized and wanted to keep up the habit.

A friend introduced me to a wonderful workout facility. It was small, intimate, and we worked hard at interval training. We had one segment where we slammed a heavy ball. I used to pretend his picture was on the floor when I slammed the ball. It was good comedic relief during our workouts. I am almost certain that I was in a hurry to date because I was finally feeling comfortable in my own skin. Many nights, I wasted time preparing for dates and listening to stories of ex-wives.

I have been described as an empath. What a recipe for disaster. I gave so much of me and my attention to *their* (my dates) lives. It was my life that needed more attention. I wish I had a do-over. I would have kept so much more energy for myself to grow and become stronger. I can say I gained no value from dating during the numbing stage. I did not think it through or value my own self-worth of what I had to offer.I was unable to give my whole heart away. I do not think there is any set amount of time anyone can project that is appropriate for healing. There is not a rulebook for a timeline of healing. For me, it was hard to heal my soul with the PFEF attacks that went on for literally years. I had to endure consistent pain, fear, and insistent attacks. I had to show my ex-husband respect and kindness, regardless of what was happening to me. He is their father, and they love him. And that is what is most important. The truth is our children will not fully understand the depth of what transpired until they have their own loves. I had to forgive their dad during the attacks.

At present, we are seven and a half years severed as a family. In 2016, after four years of wasted dating energy and the purple fish war, I took an emotional break from *any desire t*o date. I realized my loving energy was being exasperated on *any* date or yet, any quest for a date. I began to pray for God to send me a Godly man, partner, or perhaps husband. I envisioned him humble, grateful, and true to my inner being. My fun friend says I want the Hallmark Movie. *I do!* No pun there!

I started to feel the maturation of my self-respect internally. I remember, as my daughter grew, my standards for myself grew. I formulated a stance. I asked myself, *"Would you want your daughter to act this way? Would you want a man to treat your daughter this way?"*. I posed this question to my close friends. I could feel this resonating with them. I conducted myself with this inspiration. This had and continues to have a grand impact on my behavior. It helped me from losing my self-respect during a difficult transition while dating. Upon grounding myself regarding what was important to me, my self-value, self-worth, and personal standards changed. I was closely surrounded by friends that inspired me by their actions and relationships with God.

Five years post-separation, and fully divorced, I thought I met the man I had been praying for. We had an instant connection. Our first correspondence was through business. Neither of us was thinking of dating at the time. He truly had me at "*Hello.*" For months, we had a sweet friendship via telephone prior to meeting in person. He was extremely helpful in guiding me with parenting. My situation was extremely stressful, given my children's ages and the PFEF disfunction. He was a kind friend who helped me through difficult times, solely via telephone. Each conversation led us to become more intellectually close. We genuinely liked each other. We were so happy to talk to each other.

At our first face to face meeting, I fell *supercalifragilistic* in love with him. He also fell *expialidociously* in love with me. He was sincere, patient, funny, handsome, caring, funny, full of wisdom, funny, and handy. Did I say funny? He was extremely close to his children, along with his extended family. He loved his mama, and this was so important and appealing to me. My ex-husband had no relationship with his mother. In fact, he was estranged from his

family at a young age. I decided early on in my newfound singlehood; I simply would not date a man who was not close or kind to his mother.

My man instantly bonded with my children. Naturally, this felt so soothing for my children to witness this type of a man who cared about their mom. He honored God. I was certain; he was the man I prayed so long for. However, he was bound to another woman by a piece of paper, a biblical/spiritual/legal piece of paper. I had my personal rule, do not date a separated man. We became engaged rather quickly after we met. The fact he was not legally divorced went against my core belief of dating. We fell in love (*I believe at hello*), and I allowed him into my life due to his circumstances. We both believed it would be a quick paper filing, and the divorce would be behind him and us in a few short months.

As much as I was supposed to handle parenting by myself, when my fiancé jumped in, he helped handle the situation eloquently. Keep in mind, we were long-distance and our time together with my children was short due to his close family members who, very sadly, had declining health. It was difficult for us to be in the same state physically. Our time spent with my children was enjoyable, more structured than ever, and my children responded very well to the family life we tried to give them. Our relationship with each other was soothing and sometimes euphoric. We helped each other grow. We loved being in the same space together. We encompassed our entrepreneurial spirit. Music played a huge role and created a bond from our very first few conversations. He was the most favorite coffee partner I could ever ask for. We talked about God often, and he led me closer to the bible. I admired his views on God and life in general. I respected him as an individual and a human being. He loved me for the woman I am, including my flaws. He dealt with my flaws in such a smooth stride. He was

IT for me. I loved him and nurtured him, something he was not used to. I loved him the most I could, given our long-distance situation.

Three years have passed, that official paper he originally told me would be so easy to obtain, does not exist. There is no signature. (*I feel like the burger-meister – meister-burger*). I broke my own rule in my own home.

One year after dating, he paused our relationship. He decided to refrain from visiting me and my children. He felt this was best. We maintained our relationship via modern technology. The kids and I were constantly waiting for him to visit and obtain his divorce. Despite his efforts and all our eager anticipation, his divorce was never finalized. I had to shift my perspective in all the realms of my career, children, and love. I dove deeper into my core values. I realized I compromised myself both emotionally and spiritually. I exposed my children to *exactly* what I did not want them to witness, which was a man in and out of my life (auuuuugh).

I was in love with a man waiting for a piece of paper. This was not how I should have valued my life and my love. My advice is, do not date a separated man. You cannot be prepared for all the emotional trains on the track. A separated man is ***not*** yours to date. He is still literally married in the eyes of God. I needed to be stronger emotionally after my divorce. I needed to be ready to date purposefully. I was extremely selective regarding who would ever make the cut to be part of our family. I am grateful for that. However, by compromising, I led my children through the roller coaster of now you see him, now you don't.

I had to stay true to what I believed in. I learned how to listen to my own voice of intuition and the Holy Spirit. I became strong and confident to know that a separated man was not my dream nor healthy for my children or me, despite how much I loved and still love him. Every one of us is unique, and all situations are different.

There are no rules for falling in love, except loving yourself. At present, we are no longer together. I am filing this under *"H"* for heartbreak. There is an excerpt that I and my cousins cherish from my (missed and loved) late Aunt's favorite poem.

> *"You plant your own garden and decorate your own soul.*
> *Instead of waiting and waiting for someone to bring you*
> *flowers."- Jorge Luis Borges*

I lost my friend and my love, the special man I thought was divine. The only choice I have is to handle my heartache like a strong woman, for me, and especially for my children. I understand that God has a plan for our journeys. The significance here is when you allow someone in your life, it is not just you that will be affected. It is you and your children. It cannot be a selfish decision. Know that when you let a man in, you open vulnerability to your children's hearts. Children yearn for structure and stability. When we as single moms let any man in and potentially playhouse, we are taking their sense of family stability and playing with it again, sorry. I cannot say I regret my circumstances. We were careful with the morals and boundaries we placed around my children.

Dream Builder

As I desired to be a better human and make better decisions, a short nine months ago, I discovered the *Dream Builder* program. I thought I discovered it by accident or perhaps not. An airline friend, whom I kept in touch periodically, embarked on a new career endeavor. He asked me to accept a free coaching call. I had NO DESIRE to listen. I felt I knew everything that he had to present. After all, I carried a keen awareness of being positive and keeping a great attitude for things to fall into place. I am in my

12th year of business, and, at times, I had $13.00 in the checking account. I knew how to stay the course and persisted with faith in God that I could make this career work for my family. I chose Esthetics because I had a huge passion for the industry. While 20 years young, I successfully sought a career in the airline industry; hence I became a ticket/everything agent.

Our airline family named me, "President of the Hair and Nails Club", and here I am now with my own skincare boutique. I remember driving pushbacks for 737's. Thinking back, I consider myself bad to the bone. We have sustained our friendships for 35 years, and they are part of my tribe that continues to support and strengthen me.

I was certain I could teach what he had to present. I told him, *"Yeah, yeah, yeah I know all about it"*. To be kind, I took an hour to listen to his presentation. Something resonated with me, and I joined a program that remodeled my life. I did something kind for him, and it resulted in helping so many aspects of my life and others in my circle.

Since entering this program, I experienced a change in the PFEF's attitude. I believe the shift in my ex-husband's behavior is due to the shift in my thought process and outlook. I am aware that his shift is a temporary state of mind that does not last long. I had worked diligently with written exercises of forgiveness for my ex-husband. It transcribed great therapeutic thinking and writing. This work helped me truly forgive my ex despite his continual harmful behavior. Since implementing this life-changing program, many benefits are flowing. I have learned to walk stronger in my faith. I have learned to be a better mom by shifting my thought process regarding how I handle their behaviors. Ohhhhhh, mommy guilt, you really have no place here now.

The road to age 54 has allowed me to understand the paradigms (beliefs we tell ourselves) that have debilitated me more than I ever realized. While implementing new thought processes, I acquired more energy and serenity to achieve the basic wants and hopes that I keep. I have been able to implore, more than ever, the realization that God wants happiness for us. When I cleared false paradigms, (continuous false beliefs), I understood that continually hanging onto situations and thoughts that I assumed would make me feel safe, is exactly the opposite of what makes me flourish.

I have more emotional freedom than I thought possible. By nature, others view my persona as emotional. **We can be emotional, even if men do not always understand it.** A PFEF will tell you how wrong it is. It is not wrong. It is the false thoughts in our heads that get in our way. I highly encourage you to seek out a program with a coach that can aide you through the low self-esteem, fear, and significant worry that can bind itself to a divorced woman. The verbal self-destruction that we employ to ourselves does not serve us. It is a tall (*should I say Venti*) order to occupy the role of divorced mom and single owner/operator entrepreneur while hoping to continue to give your children all that a husband/wife team can. As the sign on my windowsill states, *"The house was clean yesterday, sorry you missed it"*.

By changing *my thoughts* and surrounding myself with like-minded people, I can get into a groove to keep the momentum of clarity and happiness. I have a partner in believing (one of my best friends), and we have supported each other daily in our quests to be a better version of ourselves and reach for the Holy Spirit more. Least I forget to mention coffee, how could I forget a key component?

In my instance, it was the *Dream Builder* program, along with my amazing, sincere coach that has led me to a better life path. I encourage you to find a steady stream of positive thoughts, chasing away the negative noise and destruction in your head. There is a plethora of programs, books, CDs, and apps available that are free to utilize. This will help you develop into a total flourishing mom and human being. It is the daily work that can keep you strong.

I had to fight through emotion and fully realize God does want good things for us. When we are stuck in a situation where someone is continually harming us or trying to harm us, for our children's sake, it is imperative to decline giving energy or validity to situations harmful or toxic in your life. I stress, I thought I was doing a good job with keeping my feelings private and keeping my children out of the hate and disdain my ex demonstrated for me. I did not. I did not come close to how stoic-like I should have reacted. I am not the same person today as when I was asked to walk away from that marriage seven years ago.

My hope is that I can encourage women to quickly get out of the trap of defending or explaining to your ex *or* your children. I cannot tell you the years (***and I mean years***), I explained to my children, the what's, why's, and how's of my actions.

While contemplating leaving a marriage that does not feel great to you, remember, this decision will greatly affect your children. Children do not enjoy divorce. They love their mother and father, and they want to love both freely. They desire their family to stay together. It is all they know. I think you will find great value by seeking out yourself first. Did you love in a manner lined up with God? Did you both seek counseling or ways to improve yourselves and your union? Is there hope for repair? There is no easy, smooth path after divorce, especially with small children. At times, it can be brutal.

As you become more confident in your self-worth and your faith, your energies will begin to shift. Changes will occur naturally. Peace and harmony can reside more in your family dynamic. The insight will be progressively clearer and more profound as you make your decisions regarding healthy choices for you, your children, and your future. I know because it has shifted for me, especially in the last nine months. I have been more aware of God's desires and more grateful for the abundance surrounding us. Because I have worked so deliberately and on purpose with these principles, my relationship with my ex has become more tolerable. He is less finger-pointing, and I have learned to be much less reactive. This is much healthier for our children.

Divorce can age you. It was draining. I knew I had to emphasize self-care. I needed help more than I realized. Self-care is directly related to self-talk. Self-care is directly related to us. I worked out, ate properly, exercised, and slept well. However, when I had conversations with myself, pointing out my flaws, continually addressing what I did not like, it directly interceded with the potential of the woman, the parent, and the entrepreneur I could be. What does pointing out my flaws, failures (needed them to learn and prosper), cellulite, flabby arms, and my big fat vein do for me? Oh, by the way, the vein enabled me to birth, my children. *You get it, no vein, no children.* How does the focus on any of this help me empower my desire, worth, or value? It does not, period. Negative self-talk is the undertow. It is dangerous and can hurt us. I needed to stay out of the danger of the undertow.

Conclusion

During my marriage and throughout my divorced years, the PFEF challenged my every thought and action. It was one of the PFEF's dominant traits. I did not realize it until the end of my marriage. Regretfully, I spent a lot of my time defending myself. The upside is I did not speak of my actions once I departed. I saved so much grief for myself.

It takes a great deal of effort to run the marathon I run. It was much harder when my little ones were, well, little. I often speak about how much a woman must accomplish to keep up with herself and her health. We have such a long list. I try to keep up. I am the Esthetician who instills in others the importance of our nighttime skincare routine. I am still trying to conquer that one for myself. I had so many close friends that surrounded me while I faced criminal charges. I had so many caring people, near and far, supporting me through as I mothered my children.

It is imperative you surround yourself with a tribe (your trusted group of close friends or family) who can support, guide, and lift you up. Your tribe should share your values. You should be able to respect their actions and beliefs. Divorce is difficult. It elevates to the 10th power when you are involved with an ex who possesses a personality disorder. Seek and pray for your healthy tribe! I began to improve significantly, lining up with what I believed from my inner core. I followed the principles of not inviting a dating interest into my home. I knew I needed to keep an emotional distance and physical distance from anyone I dated. It is happenstance that a dating situation can escalate too quickly. I created my plan of action. Be selective with who you supply your energy. Decipher who you can heal and grow with. Between my single besties and my own experience, I think I might puke if I must ponder another man's relationship with his ex. Seriously, I am talking vomit. Preserve your energy and give life to *your* dreams and aspirations. You must become selfish to become stronger.

I have been told; I am a new person. I explain that I am still me, with an acquired, grounded, positive outlook, and a grandeur state of gratitude. A friend asked, "how do you get through (*insert topic*) when it hurts you?". I realized that my newfound gratitude *in* the situations in my life has given me the strength through the tough moments. I have come to rely on God more and to reach deeper for the Holy Spirit's guidance. I have always heavily relied on intuition. However, after learning how to understand and deal with my false paradigms, I placed them in a reality check. I taught myself not to disburse my energy or attention more than two minutes (maybe three to five) without shifting to a different vibe and healthier mindset.

Take Backs

- Fleeing a situation can leave you broken, scared, vulnerable, questioning what you have done, and at times fill your head with negative self-talk. I wish you the knowhow to be good to yourself. You can get to a healthier place faster, regardless of your circumstances. Your new beginning can be fulfilling, sprinkled with love and gratitude.

- It is my hope that you have metaphorically and emotionally traveled with me through my journey. My hope is that you know your value and learn how to become whole through whatever channels you need. I will tell you, complaining about your ex and rehashing his behavior will keep you in a loop, *round like a circle, like a wheel within a wheel, never-ending or beginning on an ever-spinning wheel.* Do you remember this song?

- Forgiveness is essential. It is the oxygen to heal and move forward. I had the job of dodging criminal charges, raising my children with full custody as a single mom, all while outwardly respecting their father and trying to forgive him. I had four tasks to accomplish simultaneously. I know now why my sister gave me a wonder-woman t-shirt for my birthday.

- Forgiveness is compared to electricity, water, and Wi-Fi. We cannot live fully without it! It was my obligation to both repair and improve my family unit. I recently went through exercises that helped me forgive all that has transpired to myself and my children. Forgiveness remedies your soul. It frees up space to allow love and prosperity to flow. I learned forgiveness is essential for yourself. I had to find ways to let go of my pain. The sooner I did, the sooner I prospered. I used a method of writing out my thoughts. I wrote a list describing my likes and dislikes regarding my ex. It was extremely clearing for me. This is something I learned from my coaching program. It is a wonderful mindset to guide you through difficult circumstances and situations. It is also another way to lean on God more consistently.

- Shifting your thoughts to healthier outcomes, praying, and forgiving (remember I had to keep forgiving while it was happening to me and my children), will help you climb up your stronger mountain to stand on.

- Your career will require much from you. It does not segregate. Realize, there will be roadblocks, speedbumps, construction, and bridges out. Seriously, get on autopay for your electric bill. Just do it. Otherwise, the power goes out. My point is your career requires you to be *on*. It is essential to ground yourself, preferably each morning. You must be emotionally ready and even more important, grounded and refreshed for the entire workload that it takes to be a single mompreneur.

- I love to listen to music with healing binaural beats during my day. I use YouTube as a free source. It is just imperative that you have a morning start with strong, healing, and strengthening energy.

- I sign up for a bible verse that comes to me via email each morning. This is helpful, too. I only started this consistent mindset nine months ago. I wish I had implemented these tools or had the wherewithal to stop and ground myself in the cyclone of emotional abuse.

♥ A huge, monumental suggestion is to not give the abusive behavior a garden to grow. We ruminate over the behavior, the verbal attacks, and the pain it causes. Again, as I have learned, there is no value in spreading the words of the verbal attacks. When one is experiencing it, it is a natural response because it hurts; it bruises and can be scary, to say least. However, the "*look what he did*" mentality does not serve us. The less we focus our attention on it, the more we have time to heal from it. I am living proof that the attacks keep happening, and I understand you just want to get off this ride. Your advantage point is to change your channel.

♥ I am learning and discovering, seven years post-separation and divorce, about the paradigms that emotionally held me back *(some since age 12)*. Some of you, perhaps, could be stuck in fear or thoughts that can hold you back and keep you from expanding and growing on many variable levels. False paradigms *can* leave you frozen and keep you steadily on a hamster wheel. It makes me think of the song, *"Will it go around in circles" (by Billy Preston).*

♥ Remember, God is always present with us. He sends His Holy Spirit to comfort and guide us. I encourage you to dig deep and connect with Him. Realizing all the trials, tribulations, and blessings around us, is part of the strength to help us through life and our purpose. God is love, and we must continue to love because that is why he created us.

Love is patient; love is kind. It does not envy; it does not boast; it is not proud. It does not dishonor others; it is not self-seeking; it is not easily angered; it keeps no record of wrongs. Love does not delight in evil but rejoices with the truth. It always protects, always trusts, always hopes, always perseveres. Love never fails. But where there are prophecies, they will cease; where there are tongues, they will be stilled; where there is knowledge, it will pass away. For we know in part and we prophesy in part, but when completeness comes, what is in part disappears. When I was a child, I talked like a child, I thought like a child, I reasoned like a child. When I became a man, I put the ways of childhood behind me. For now, we see only a reflection as in a mirror; then we shall see face to face. Now I know in part; then I shall know fully, even as I am fully known.

And now these three remain faith, hope, and love. But the greatest of these is love.

1 Corinthians 13; 4-13, NIV

Teresa Robinson

trobinsonbooks@yahoo.com

Taking broken hearts caused by "Once Upon A Times" and empowering women is one example of Teresa Robinson's love of God's truths and writing. Teresa is a career educator whose passion is working with college students and women, encouraging them to see that the windshield of life is larger than the rearview mirror. She also strives to empower women of all ages through celebrating their special gifts and God's love for them.

Teresa and her husband Doug, have four daughters and two granddaughters they hope will always know how "royal" they are. They also have four sons and three grandsons who they hope will understand the importance of God's role in their lives.

Favorite Scripture

Ephesians 4:32
Be kind and compassionate to one another, forgiving each other,
just as in Christ God forgave you.

Dedication

I dedicate my chapter to my children who overcame divorce with a spirit of love and determination, my friends and family who fought lovingly to keep me from losing sight of the finish line, my husband for being my true Knight in Shining Armor, and to my Heavenly Father for the true meaning of love.

The Truth About Fairytales

By: Teresa Robinson

Once upon a time, in a land far away, there was a prince and a princess whose childhood years were spent growing up and learning about life together. Following graduation, the pair ventured off to college together, and two years following graduation, they were married. After they established their kingdom, the new King and Queen spent a few years traveling, meeting new friends, and settling into careers. Life was mostly carefree and adventurous. In time, two little princesses and a prince were born, and all seemed happy and perfect. Sixteen years after their fairy tale wedding, dark days set upon the kingdom when the King rode off from the palace to marry someone from another kingdom.

Okay. Enough with the fairy tale lingo. I am sure you get the picture of what happened in my marriage. My situation was not uniquely different than what many others go through. This may mirror a time you have gone through or are going through now, or perhaps your situation may be different. Regardless of the cause of your separation and divorce, the pain and confusion you are feeling is experienced and shared by many and seems nothing remotely like the, "Once Upon A Time," that you had once hoped for when you began your marriage. Later, I will talk more about the "Truth about Fairy Tales" because I feel very strongly about what the Bible says about this. First, I want to share how I survived those dark days, weeks, and months when my life as I knew it all changed. Life was already a juggling act with three children and a full-time job teaching. Then unexpectedly, I had to add the element of fear in the form of the question, "Where do I go from here?" All I really wanted to do is stop the world and get off. Living happily ever after or even living happily at all was difficult to imagine.

Looking back at this time, I learned so much about life and myself. I remember saying once during the chaos that I hoped I lived to be old and wise, so one day, I might understand why people do what they do. To be honest, I do not think I could ever live long enough to accomplish this, and I do not think we are meant to figure others out. Polishing ourselves to be all we can be takes enough time and effort. There is little time to try to worry about the flaws and actions of others, although I am sure that someone else's flaws are central in your mind now. But one thing I want you to hear me say is, wherever you are now in your journey, healing and peace will come. I believe that with all my heart. Dear friends, I do not know where you are in your journey. The pain, anger, and loneliness may be fresh and raw. Maybe the time has passed and has begun to dull the ache a bit. Wherever you are, I hope that by sharing bits of my story, you will see a pathway to peace.

The finish line may seem unreachable at this time. I remember that time all too well. Hang on! With God's guiding hand and your faith, you will reach that place. I wish I had stories like these in, "Still Standing" to read and offer me hope when I was going through my divorce. Few of my friends had experience with divorce, and for that, I am very thankful. Not having many friends with this type of experience to lean on, I had to figure most out on my own. You are taking steps to reach out and seek advice from sisters who have waded through these often-turbulent waters and walked these rocky roads. We have figured some things out for you. I pray that our words will help lead you through your journey with our Lord's guiding hand. We are still standing, and we want you to be standing strong and tall right beside us.

Once Upon a Time Years

All stories, like fairy tales, have beginnings, middles, and endings. More than likely, the beginning of the story of your marriage was full of joy and hope. The wedding industry makes billions of dollars a year in magazine sales, photography businesses, flowers, honeymoon packages, and everything a couple needs for their marriage to have a grand start. Our expectations are hopeful for these lives we are beginning. The first years of our lives as newlyweds, these "Once Upon A Time" years, may have had some small bumps, but for the most part, they were more than likely happy and full of hope. My beginning chapters, my "Once Upon a Time" years, were not perfect, but I was happy, and when those times came along that were not quite so rosy, there were enough positive things to bring back happiness. It is these "Once Upon a Times" that haunt us as we begin to move through the shadows of the day to day of our new lives.

When I was alone at night after my ex-husband left, I remember thinking about those times. I was haunted by memories of our dating years, our college years together, the babies, family vacations, and all of those things that started the foundation of our time together: our story. Our relationship began the summer after our junior year in high school. This ran into four years of college. After a year of breaking up and seeing other people, we found our way back together, became engaged, and married. I believe all these thoughts ached so much because there was so much loss in these memories. As a mother, I knew my children would be so wounded, and this broke my heart. I also knew they would lose those special family traditions we had chosen to create that were the foundation of their young lives.

As a woman, I felt left out and at a loss of how to piece life back together for all of us. The fairy tale ended, and instead of closing the book and choosing something else to read, I became entangled in this story, and it just continued like a bad dream that I could not wake up from. The beginning chapters of our marriage ended much too soon.

The years since my divorce, I have had the privilege of meeting and talking with many women who are going through separation or divorce. One of my hopes is that I have been able to offer them some hope as they have moved from the "Once Upon a Time" of their story to these middle chapters of their story. It is these middle chapters where the painful experiences are. These chapters may be where you are now. How do you put into words what you cannot understand, as you begin to live out this part of your life's story? I remember feeling like I was lost in a maze. I had no idea which direction or road to take. There were voices everywhere telling me what I should do, then at times, there was only silence. At this time of my life, before the separation, things had become busy and complicated in our lives. We had three children, the youngest being only two years old, and both of us had demanding careers. I felt alone many times, and looking back, I knew things were not what they should be for us as a couple, but I never expected a divorce. We had a history together. We had just built a new house in a new town. I was always hopeful the days would get better for us. That just was not the case. He told me in October he wanted to leave. A few weeks later, he moved out. Our divorce became final March of the following year. A relationship that took over 20 years to build took only a few weeks to crumble and less than six months to end.

Journaling

Very early in my separation, a friend encouraged me to keep a Journal. This friend had suffered through a divorce years before and had later found happiness and love again. I cannot tell you how much this simple suggestion helped me. In my journals, I could fuss, write bad words, write letters that would never be sent, write poetry (I never knew I could write poetry), and plan death scenarios (just being honest). Journaling offered me such release, and the greatest part was I could go back months later and reread what I had written, and I could say, "Oh, that poor girl. She was a mess. Look how far she has come." It was on these pages that I wrote when I did not have the strength to talk or when I had no idea what I was even feeling.

Being a teacher for many years, I had witnessed families and had conferences with parents who were going through or had gone through a divorce. Some quietly explained their situations, and I felt encouraged by the way they were determined to work through their pain to protect their children. Sadly, however, more often, I encountered those so full of anger, and their children were front row and center to all that the parents were experiencing. As a result, their children were experiencing it, too. At that time, of course, I had no idea what they were going through and hoped never to know. However, I made a mental note after hearing each story to remember how differently each child was going to be affected due to the parents' reactions.

In my journals, I wrote about some of these memories, these snapshots of lessons I learned from other families, that I now needed to remember for my own family. Other peoples' pain has always bothered me deeply, and I was always haunted by some of the family stories I heard through these conferences. I could also "read" on each child's face the story being played out in

their homes. I am especially thankful that I took the time to listen to these families both to help their children while they were in my classroom and later to use those valuable lessons to take care of my own sweet children. These are some of the types of stories and other personal ideas I wrote in my journals instead of talking about them. Keeping thoughts and feelings bottled up is not healthy, but constantly bombarding everyone with a story full of anger and sadness is not either. I encourage you to start a journal if you have not yet. One day it will chronicle your own testimony of survival to assist you in helping others. While you are going through this pain now, writing will help clear your mind. As you write, it will help your wounded heart see hope.

In one of my journals, very early in the separation phase, I wrote the following words:

"I wonder how long it will take me to get over this. I've never really heard anyone say. Each day is like a bad dream in slow motion. I'm afraid and sad and lonely."

One of the things I remembered as I re-read my journals to prepare to write this chapter is that I wrote quite a few poems during the first year of separation and divorce. This was new for me and totally unplanned. Sometimes the words just flowed, and I wrote them as they poured from my heart. Day-to-day living took all I had most of the time as I began this new life. Tasks were so numerous, time seemed never to be enough, and yet no one knew my struggle. I wanted to cry and ask, "Does anyone know?" as I walked through my days and began walking the road that I hoped would eventually lead to peace and healing.

Does Anyone Know

Does anyone know the pain I feel?
Just making coffee, bathing kids, walking the dog
Does anyone know?
Can anyone hear my cries?
That echo through my soul
The cries of pain and loneliness
The cries of love lost
The cries of sadness-hollow, deep
Can anyone hear?
Does anybody know?
Will there be a day when I can honestly smile at the sun and clouds?
When I can go through my day
With joy in my stride, Joy in my heart
Does anybody know?
Does anyone know?
Will I able to reach out to others, offer them hope?
Will I survive this day-this pain-this hour- to love again?
Does anyone know?
Does he know what he has caused?
The pain, confusion, desperation.
The me who simply exists each day, the shell of a person
Raising kids, working, fighting to eat, fighting to sleep.
Does he know? Does he care?
Does he feel anything at all?
I know the One who cares
The One who will continue to love me and lift me from these shadows.
The One from Whom all goodness comes
Lift me Lord, so I may find happiness, peace, joy
A purpose to finish the race- to want to live life again.

As I read this poem that I had written so many years ago and chose it to share with you, even after 16 years, those feelings I had so long ago stirred ever so vividly. Verse by verse, the poem told a story of my day to day life at that time. Doing simple tasks like making coffee sometimes felt like a chore. Many times, I remember feeling like I had weights strapped to my legs, trying to carry them around as I went about my day.

> *Does anybody know?*
> *Will there be a day?*
> *When I can honestly*
> *Smile at the sun and clouds*
> *When I can go through my day*
> *With joy in my stride*
> *Joy in my heart*
> *Does anybody know?*

This stanza especially rang out to me as I read it all these years later. I remember needing to know if things were ever going to get better. Would I ever wake up, and my feet touch the floor, and something else storm into my mind besides the divorce and all the baggage that went along with it? How long would I feel lost and plain sad?

I was always such a happy person. I wanted that person back. Would she ever be back like she was, or would a broken person replace her? I did not want to be a broken person, and I wanted someone to be able to help me understand all my fears. Can you relate? Honestly, I had forgotten these feelings until I read them in my journal. I hope that gives you faith that time does dull the memories and the pain of the events that hurt us so terribly while going through separation and divorce.

The Middle Chapters and Lessons Learned

Now let us begin to take a walk through these middle chapters of separation and divorce together. In a fairy tale, this is where the details of the story would unfold as well as the problem, and rising actions would occur. In real life, some days, the road you are walking will seem rough and full of potholes and scary places. Do any of those places sound familiar already? How about the days of finding out all the secrets? How about telling your children, seeing the pain on their faces, and hearing their cries? Even if you do not have children, for all of us, telling family members and friends is painful, too. These haunting visions and sounds do not disappear easily or quickly, if ever. The beginning days of our middle chapters that eventually lead to divorce hurt about as much as anything I could ever imagine. It seems that there is something new around every corner that you do not want to find out about or do not want to hear. Being lost in a foggy maze for days at a time is how I felt. I had to keep going. I had to keep functioning. Questions upon questions flooded my mind, but for the most part, I wanted no answers. Clearly, I remember staring at the face of this person I had known since middle school, yet he seemed to move backward down a funnel of some sort. He looked different. His voice was different. What was he saying? I had to really listen to make sense of his words. Did he really mean those things he was saying to me? Me? The person who had been through so much with him?

How about all of those "firsts?" First holidays and birthdays cause fear and sadness like nothing else. You may be facing those times now. While reading my journals, three of these firsts stood out. One of the entries centered on how much I was dreading Thanksgiving because I was going to be alone that day. This was the first major holiday I would have as a single person. In the separation agreement, I allowed the children to go with their father on Thanksgiving holidays if he continued to hold the same traditions because we always celebrated with his extended family. I wanted the kids to keep their traditions. This was also important to me because I loved and missed his family so much. However, in my journal, I wrote, *"I refuse to waste four days worrying about one day that will be over before I know it."* So, I was determined to keep my mind focused on living out Sunday through Wednesday with my children and friends and put Thursday out of my mind.

God puts special messages in His Word when we need it. The scripture that appeared during my devotion time on one of these days was, Job 37:14: *"...stop and consider God's wonders."* I remember thinking how random a scripture from Job was when I was reading the devotion that day. I also remember the peace I felt when I looked the verse up and read those words.

This will not be the last time I mention this truth of scripture appearing at the perfect time. God's Word truly speaks right to you when you listen to what He wants to say to you. Those days were much easier to face keeping this in mind. I treasured the wonders of my kids' excitement about being out of school for the holiday.

I treasured the wonder of their excitement to see their family. We made fun Thanksgiving food and crafts. We were thankful and enjoyed the week together. However, Thursday finally rolled around and still caught me totally, emotionally unprepared.

I clearly remember that first Thanksgiving Day. It was tough. Correction, it was not tough; it was just plain awful. To be fair, many friends invited me to their homes for the holiday, but I chose to be alone, so most of the blame I now put on myself. What made me think this was a good idea, I am not sure.

Thanksgiving that year for me was spent sitting at home alone watching "Gone with the Wind" of all things. How uplifting was that? Play by play of what I knew was going on during their Thanksgiving celebration was going on in my mind while I sat in the darkened family room watching a movie, I cared nothing about. In hindsight, both were a major mistake on my part. Hopefully, you can see that I should have taken an offer from a friend instead of sitting in a house alone. The children were worried about me being alone, too, despite the happy face I put on and the fun things we did to celebrate being thankful before they left for the day. Lessons were learned from this first holiday. I learned a hard lesson, that a holiday is no day for a pity party. It is not healthy for anyone and is an incredible waste of a day. The scripture that helped me to prepare so much for the day would have helped me so much on that day, but I chose to bury it away. This was definitely a day of lessons for me, and now I am "thankful" for those lessons.

The first Christmas was difficult, too. On December 21st, I wrote in my Journal,

"It seems like a very short time ago I wrote 66 days until Christmas and I was dreading it so. I'm doing surprisingly well, though.

Although waves of sadness pass through me, I guess, for the most part, I have accepted things and am moving on in the respect that I know I have done all I can do. He made his choice, and I've got to believe that somehow I will be better off this way."

Our family always had sweet traditions and fun celebrations built around our children. That first year, I worked very hard and kept things the same. Together, the children and I ventured out and purchased a live tree just as we always had. After we returned home, we decorated it with all of the trimmings and enjoyed hot chocolate and cookies like they had grown used to. Decorations were placed exactly where they were always placed. Counting down to Christmas looked like any other Christmas at our house. Or at least that is what I hoped. I guess maybe I had hoped he would come in to visit the kids and see our home and change his mind. I know I wanted the kids to be secure and see that not everything had changed in their lives. My guess now is that I wanted a little of both.

Even though I thought I was beginning to accept things as they were going to be, it was at this point that I began to fear that I would always be alone. I felt lonely, and it scared me. While Christmas shopping, I was acutely aware of couples shopping together. It seemed like everyone had someone, and I was shopping alone. Realistically I knew this was not the truth but, everyone except couples seemed to fade into the background as I walked through the mall. This loneliness was the hardest part of separation and divorce for me, and it was at its most painful that first Christmas. I am sure the festivities of the holidays and the millions of tasks a parent must do, kept my mind somewhat occupied through this season. Honestly, I remember very little about this Christmas Day. Pictures show many smiles, and the children looked happy. As usual, I am absent from most of the pictures since I am usually the photographer, but the pictures mirror Christmases from before. It all seemed happy and "normal".

My sister is always the life of the party, and she was that day. She and my dad were and still are such vital constants for my kids and me. Because of their love and presence all the time, especially that first year, it was hard to miss who was not there, but I am sure the ghost of the one missing was still present.

The third "first" was my birthday. My first birthday single happened to be my 40th. As if turning 40 was not hard enough, to add insult to injury, I was a divorced mother of three on this milestone birthday. Although I had learned a lesson at

Thanksgiving, somewhere between November and August, I seemed to have forgotten that important lesson I had learned. So again, I chose to be alone on my birthday, so I did not have to face the "party". My two daughters spent the day and evening with my sister. My little boy went to bed at 8:00. Just like before, I found myself alone and wondering why. The next day, my sister showed up with my kids and a cake with so many candles on it that it set off the smoke detector in our living room! We laughed until we cried. I laughed, and it felt good; good to laugh, and good to celebrate with people who wanted to celebrate me.

These "firsts" passed with me surviving despite myself. As stubborn and as hard-headed as I had been, lessons learned did finally get through to me, and the lessons began to stick. On future holidays and special occasions, I chose not to do things alone as much, and I made deliberate choices to make things less painful on myself. These words I had written in my Journal also stood out to me after these firsts:

"Many firsts are now behind me. I'm proud of myself. I've cried a little. No. I've cried a lot. I've lost some weight and have been sad, but I've handled it all with grace and dignity, and hopefully, I will be a better person for surviving these storms".

Middle Chapters

Unexpected Friendships and Blessings

As you are walking through these days of "firsts" or whenever you are facing days filled with pain and uncertainty in the middle chapters of this journey, there are some definite dos and dont's. I have mentioned some of the dont's, but the other side is even more important. To begin, do find something constructive and busy to do. Do stay away from the radio. It is not your friend. Do be selective about movies you see and the books you read. Most of all, do trust God and wise friends to help you through these dark and lonely times. It is the wisdom and the light of God that will guide you down these roads.

Some days in the middle chapters of your story you may feel gray, desperate, and lonely. Because of these feelings, it will seem like you are the only one traveling the road. For me, those days were the hardest, as I had mentioned. I felt like I could battle anything except the ache of loneliness. Most of the memories I have of the separation and divorce were those of being lonely and just plain lost. Oh, I put on a good show. My children never saw me cry and never heard me say anything unkind about the entire situation. I had five friends who were my "go-to" people whom I could share with at any time and two of those were praying partners. I forever will be blessed by those two ladies and others who helped pray away so much heartache. Three were my "partners in crime". The second set was harmless, but it was good to have friends to vent to and who would go right along with me and my rants and crazy notions, especially on my worst days. There are some fun, and crazy memories that we can still laugh about that helped me so much through these dreary days that were my norm at that time. What a blessing they were and still are. No judgment; all love. What a blessing it is to have friends who love me unconditionally.

I chose not to burden my other friends or other people with my story unless someone asked. Loving people did ask. People really cared and were heartbroken right along with me. I was careful with my words and what I shared. Stories were still going to spread no matter what words were shared. Reliving the story was not pleasant, I did not want to continue to talk about it, so I chose to keep it as brief as possible. Some people find healing through talking. Find what works for you as long as it is healthy.

Reflecting on this time, my suggestion, based on what was most helpful for me is for you to develop a hobby that ends with a product like painting, stained glass, or growing things. I chose to grow herbs in my kitchen and called myself "growing through divorce". For exercise I walked at least four miles most days and ran on the treadmill while the kids were in the bath. Read Christian books. Listen to Christian music instead of music that will only make feelings worse and deliberately select movies that will make you laugh or bring happiness instead of leaving you feeling worse than before you watched them. Finally, find a Divorce Recovery or Celebrate Recovery meeting at a local church and meet others who can be there to share with you and invest in you. Find those trusted friends. Maybe this will be the time that unexpected friendships will develop, friendships that will be lifetime gifts.

Although all the suggestions so far of what you should "do" are important and helped me tremendously, the next shadows all others. Sometimes just sitting quietly and asking God to show you what to read, will allow your heart to open to hear Him speak right to you through His Word. Isaiah 30:21 is a beautiful reminder that God's voice will speak to you through scripture when you seek His guidance

Isaiah 30:21: "*Whether you turn to the right or the left, your ears will hear a voice behind you, saying, " This is the way; walk in it.*"

Invest in yourself and know that each step you take in a positive direction, will help you turn the pages of this part of your story and will help you when you are ready to begin to write the new chapters. Remember this scripture when you do not know which direction to go. He is always present and will let your path be known. Just listen for His words.

Be Intentional and Do Not Walk Alone on the Road to Recovery

My ex-husband left in October. Soon after that, I heard about a Divorce Recovery Program at a church in a neighboring town. I was encouraged by a friend to attend and to complete the program, so I did.

I learned some valuable things during this. First, I learned that many people were handling things far worse than I was. There was bitterness, anger, and extreme emotions that I did not feel, or if I did, I was not aware of them. I remember the first night of the program; the leaders showed a clip from the "Wizard of Oz" movie. For the life of me, I cannot remember now why this was shown, but it was the scene of the older woman riding her bicycle with little Toto in the basket. Almost as if it were planned, five people said at the same time, "I did not know my ex-wife was going to be here". Some folks laughed; others nodded their heads in agreement. I remember thinking that the anger was such a small part of my hurt that either I was much farther along than these people or I was not dealing with things the right way. Really, I did not know if I should be thankful or concerned.

Oh, I cannot lie. I did feel anger at different points of this journey. Remember those death scenarios I mentioned in my journal? Remember those special friends, my partners in crime? We had some pretty salty conversations early on. I am not proud of it, but I clearly remember being angry with him in certain situations.

However, the pain of not knowing why and how things had unraveled as they had, was much more of my problem than anger. After I found out that there was someone else in his life, I did not even feel angry then. The pain was too deep. The fear was too deep.

I learned a great lesson about handling anger and other negative feelings from my mother. She passed away from cancer years before this time in my life. She was a beautiful lady. I was in my early 20s, and I remember thinking she was old when she died but, age is a perspective. She was only 44 years old. I remember one day she and a friend of hers who also had cancer, dressed up and went out for a nice lunch. When I asked her why she was so dressed up for lunch, she told me she wanted people to see her for who she was, not for what problems she had. She looked at me and said these words I will never forget: "Teresa, life will not always be easy. There will be many wonderful days but some not so wonderful. Handle all days, good and bad, with grace and dignity. This will do more for you than you can imagine." Grace and dignity were not the characteristics I had in mind during these days initially, but my mother's sweet words of wisdom would be what helped move me and my family forward in the most positive direction possible.

The day the affair was discovered, and I found out the woman's name, I called a trusted friend who worked with my soon to be ex-husband and this woman. I remember trembling as I asked him if she was who I thought she was. I remember that surprise and pain in his voice when his answer was yes. I became very quiet on the phone as the reality of it all set in like a slow crushing wave. After a few seconds, he asked if I was okay. I told him I would be as I thanked him with a barely audible voice and said goodbye. Thankfully, the kids were all somewhere at that moment, so I went into my room. I did not throw things. I did not break pictures or call him and scream and yell. Listen to this, please. I dropped to my knees and prayed. Through tears, I told God I did not understand why. I did not know how things had gotten to this point but to please surround me with His love and help me handle every day ahead with grace and dignity. You see, this is why I did not carry anger with me daily. Grace and dignity helped me quietly try to figure out each day without dragging my kids through World

War III. Grace and dignity helped me not tell every poor random stranger my woes. Grace and dignity gave me the ability to survive. Grace and dignity helped me depend on the Lord instead of myself. Thank you, momma. Thank you, Lord.

How

How do you learn to exist alone?
Stop loving, Stop hating,
Stop wanting to be held and loved?
How do you learn to stop depending?
Stop wishing, Stop hoping,
Stop playing memories over and over?
How do you learn to stop being afraid?
Stop reminding yourself to breath
Stop hurting, Stop crying,
Stop wanting something so much?
How do you learn to stop dreaming?
Stop denying what is reality?
Stop feeling hopeful,
Start accepting all?
How do you learn to move on, laugh, smile?
Stop pretending and depending,
Feel less pain, feel loved again?
So much to learn
So little will...now
So much to stop
So many things to start
So many things

After the first night of the Divorce Recovery Workshop, I decided it was not for me. There were too many angry and bitter people there and how could this help me grow through my situation, were my thoughts. Still, I had promised my friend I would complete the program and yes, she reminded me of that promise. As the next Thursday night all too quickly rolled around, begrudgingly, I made my way to the meeting. Prayerfully, I drove the 20 minutes or so to the neighboring city as I began to try to explain to God all of the reasons I did not need to be away from my children and waste time at this meeting. Did you get that? I tried to explain to God the reasons. However, it did not take me long to see that indeed I needed to be there.

During this particular week's large group time, leaders shared their testimonies, and I soaked them up. Sitting there listening, I wanted to raise my hand and ask a million questions, but I just listened. During small group time, again, we were offered time to share our stories. Most did not share the first couple of weeks. Ice breaker activities allowed us to get to know each other. The goal of this was that hopefully, eventually, lines of communication would open as the weeks continued. As both men and women in our group began to open up about their experiences and their pain, I listened and heard many stories from the hurting people sitting around me. Unlike the people in a large group, these were not survivors yet. These people were like me, still trudging through the swamps of separation or divorce.

One helpful tool was the gift of the use of the "Serenity Prayer" in a large group. They provided us with a small copy and encouraged us to place this on our mirror so we would see it each morning as we were getting ready for our day. The prayer changed a bit as the weeks went on. I added the new cards to my mirror as I received them. I read them, prayed them, memorized them, and said them out loud daily. By the time the workshop was over, I was so thankful I had made the promise to my friend and took the time for myself to invest those hours a week to my recovery. I learned I was not in this boat alone. The boat was not sinking, even when it felt like it was going under. Despite the storm surge from time to time, the storm would eventually end, the seas would calm again, and once again the sun would shine, and blue skies would be visible for me.

I want you to know that this will be the same for you. You must know when to paddle your boat and when to let God take over your oars. You must also trust those people God puts in your path who tell you to hang on for those sunnier days.

Serenity Prayer

God, grant me the serenity
To accept the things, I cannot change
The Courage
To accept the things I can,
And the Wisdom to know the difference

Everything you have read comes from my experiences. It is my prayer to shorten your time of hurting and keep you from making some mistakes that could cause pain that will prevent you from healing in a timelier manner.

What I have to say next is going to sound strange, so be patient with me while you read this. Here it goes. Do not allow your happiness to be based on trying to figure out your ex or soon to be ex. Now, I know that may sound impossible. He is the cause of the pain, so how can you not try to figure out what is going on with him? This will take work and effort on your part. If you allow yourself to fixate on those things, it only opens the door for your emotions to be played with. Find a way to grow through this and stubbornly set your goals. I could write an entire book on this based on my separation alone. I can wrap it up in that one sentence I mentioned above and will mention one more time: *Do not allow your happiness to be based on trying to figure out your ex or soon to be ex.*

My pastor and his wife were close friends of mine. He gave me the best advice about just this. One day we were talking, and I kept asking, "I Wonder" questions and making "Maybe" and "What If" statements. Calmly he told me this: "Never try to imagine what your soon to be ex was thinking or feeling and never let your emotions lead you to try to figure him out". He cautioned me by explaining that I would only invent situations that were not true or, even worse, those that I would want to be true. The next words he shared really hit home. While I was spending all my time lying in bed at night with these questions and scenarios and not sleeping, my ex was sleeping and not feeling anything that I imagined him to feel. He was not losing any sleep at all. Oh, how true this is. Once I began really trying to put this into practice, his advice helped me so much; actually, it brought me peace and much-needed rest.

Remember, you know only what you know. Go with the facts. Do not let wishful wondering make things even harder for you. There will be enough things that take you by surprise that will hurt. There are enough things you already have found out that hurt. We can come up with things in our minds that hurt worse than anything that could possibly happen because we create them, wish for them, or fear them and spend valuable time "wondering" and worrying about them. Then they either do or do not come true, and that hurts even more. Women are thinkers and planners. It is who we are. We do not need to use this gift at this point. We know what we know. That is it. Protect your heart and adopt the, "Just the facts mam," philosophy. Trust me. Life will be so much easier for you.

Below are a few verses of a poem I wrote about these feelings that make this time so difficult and painful. You must give up these thoughts and feelings. This is probably the hardest phase of the early days of separation and divorce and maybe for a long time after. Wishful wonderings and hopeful hearts-they can consume us and make us feel pain deep inside where no one else can feel.

> *They say absence makes the heart grow fonder*
> *Why does it seem to only be for the one left behind?*
> *While feelings of anger and frustration and hate*
> *Should consume my heart- should force me not to feel*
> *Feelings of sadness, loneliness, heartache, and pain*
> *Consume my thoughts, my nights, and days forcing me to feel*

Not all days will be rough during this time of your healing in these middle chapters. Other days the road may be smoother and scenic, although they still will contain caution signs. These are the roads I want to concentrate on most now as we journey into, "The Truth about Fairy Tales."

Sisters, smile on those days and thank God for every blessing that you can count. If you watch, you will see blessings God has placed there just for you.

They are on the dark and lonely roads, too. On those roads, however, we are trudging along and just trying to find direction, looking down, and trying not to fall. Blessings are just easier to see when we are looking up instead of looking down.

I became a Christian when I was 11 years old. I knew my choice was real and I was thrilled when I made it. Throughout my childhood and teen years, I was a "good girl", and most of that was due to me being Baptist. I loved those older ladies at my church who sang every Sunday in the choir and looked like angels. However, just as much as I loved them, I was sure they would find a way to use one of those Baptist Hymnals upside of my head if they ever caught me doing something I should not be doing. It was good because it kept me out of trouble. It was bad because it took me from 11 years old until I was 40 years old, navigating the perils of divorce and being single, to truly realize I could never be good enough and just how much Jesus loves me; just as the song says.

Jesus really, truly, deeply, loves me, and not just when I am "good". I struggled with this fact my entire life. I just did not get the real feeling of His love and for all of those years, simply settled for living a Christian life of obedience, trying to be good, and learning what the Bible said about Christ and His love. One of the ways I chose to grow through my divorce was through reading. I read every book I could by Christian authors.

One such book was, *"Captivating"* by John and Stacy Eldredge. One of the struggles I had after going through this time was my self-worth, no big surprise. If I were special enough, why would this have happened? If…if…if. While going through my prayer time and reading this book, it finally began to dawn on me that, guess what? I am captivating to Jesus. This brought me to tears as finally, the reality of this began to weigh on me, and it felt good.

As I was sitting on my deck with my book in the quiet of the evening, I looked up from my book, remember blessings are easier to see when we look up, and on the railing right beside me landed the bluest bird I had ever seen. It just perched there on the wooden railing. My grandmother and my ex-husband's grandmother, two women I loved with all my heart, each told me every time I saw a bluebird, it meant someone loved me. Talk about tears. God's perfect timing spoke right to my heart with the sweetest message of love I had ever heard. I was beginning to understand!

Soon after that, a group of friends and I saw *"The Passion of the Christ"* right after it came out in theaters. We sat riveted, watching as the portrayal of Christ's life was unveiled in front of us. I smiled at the humanity of his sweetness as he played with his mother while he built her a table and chairs. I watched with wonder at the patience he had with some of the doubters and saw myself in so many of those people. How thankful I was for the reality of His patience in my life. In horror, I watched as they beat him until he lay on the ground in a pool of blood. When I thought there was nothing else that they could do to him and he could not stand another strike of the whip, as if he was saying he knew we would need more, he fought to stand again to offer himself for more. I cried. That scene in that moment took care of any other questions of Christ's love that I may have had. I finally got it. He is here for us when our lives seem gray and desperate, like there are four seasons of a never-ending winter or bright and cheerful like we are enjoying four seasons of spring. He loves us! Proverbs 3: 5-6 reminds us: *"Trust in the Lord with all your heart and lean not on your own understanding; in all your ways acknowledge him, and he will make your paths straight."* Now is your time to claim this and begin to trust.

Smooth days did not come as frequently as the other days did at first, but I had something now that I did not have before, and no day was ever so dark again. I looked for blessings on all roads like horses running in a field. Thank you, Jesus, for Your love. My babies were singing some goofy song just at the right time. Thank you, Jesus, for Your love. A friend was calling at the moment I really needed it. Thank you, Jesus, for Your love. Sunny and scenic roads, scary and dark roads, gray and gloomy roads, they are all a part of our journey to healing and happiness. Actually, these are a part of life, even if divorce is not a part of our journey.

Learn to see His blessings in all of your days. Your healing will happen so much faster, and your pain will hurt so much less. Be intentional. Sometimes getting out of your head, serving others, and looking for the rainbow on the other side of the clouds will make all the difference. By being intentional, you are not simply waiting for something good to happen. You are letting God and the world know that moment…that day…is yours to do good works and be happy. Take a step at a time. Turn the pages of these chapters a page at a time but turn them. Do not get stuck in this part because the best is yet to come. However, these lessons must be learned here before moving on.

Remember, I mentioned the caution signs? While you are traveling these roads and turning the pages of these middle chapters, there will be those with flashy smiles and toothy grins offering directions, shortcuts, or quick fixes for the loneliness and hard times. Trust me. They are out there, and they are sometimes hard to recognize. Oh, they may look safe. They may look like someone who can be trusted, or they may obviously look like a snake in the grass. Please remember that these people cannot offer you anything you truly need. There is no shortcut on this road. Hear that again, please. There is no shortcut on this road. Healing takes time, patience, faith, and love. At all times, stay focused on your healing, even when it is not easy, and trust those individuals God places on your path. You will know who they are. God will not put any questions in your heart about those He sends to walk with you.

There are no lefts or rights on this road to healing. If folks try to lead you on these paths instead of straight ahead, then you know they are not the people you should be following. The Bible is the roadmap we should follow at this time more than ever. Our heart has been hurt and is open to be hurt even more. Guard it and understand it needs to be guarded. This can be a difficult place to be. I met people in the divorce recovery workshop I attended who said they were trying to recover from their second relationship as much as from their divorce. I caution everyone to remember that any relationship can look good after you have been through a divorce. You have suffered a wound to your heart. That wound must be healed completely before you can reach out to another person. Getting hurt again too soon is like tearing open a wound that has not healed in the first place. It can cause even more pain the second time. I almost learned this first-hand but caught myself before I became too entangled in a situation that would have caused pain for myself and my family. I have cautioned other women. Some have listened and have thanked me. Others have not listened or have trusted those toothy smiles thinking they could trust them, and things were not what they thought they were.

Remember, we have the Bible as our guide for our understanding. Take this to heart, and your heart will know right from wrong. You can trust your heart, but you need to listen to it and not talk yourself out of what you know it is saying to you. If it feels wrong, then it probably is.

Additionally, if the voices are too much to keep straight, rely on a trusted friend to lean on when you need advice or extra encouragement. These middle chapters of your story may have been filled with ups and downs, dark days, and sadness; however, hold on. The future can be bright and better days are ahead.

Keep traveling straight ahead and claim those scriptures that I shared previously and others that are special to you. He knows the road you are on. Listen and you will hear the directions He has for you.

Lord, give me the courage
When my life is out of control
Still my heart
When it pounds so loud, it hurts
Fill my spirit with hope and love and peace
When my days seem so dark and lonely
Heal my heart so I may be a mother
A friend, a teacher who loves and smiles
Take away my sorrows of the part of my story that ended
Give me strength and courage for my new journey ahead

There will be good people God puts on your path. Sometimes they will not even be the people you are expecting. When my ex-husband left, he said there was no one else in his life. We just "didn't bring the best out in each other anymore, and he didn't love me anymore", he said. Well, there is usually more to the story, and I found out soon there was much more to our story, as I mentioned earlier. I clearly remember, the night I found out about my ex-husband's affair. With three children in my house, I had no alone time, and it was very difficult during that time to find a place to cry or simply even sort out my thoughts. A few days later, when he came to visit the kids, I drove in my car both to get away from him and just to cry. While driving, my car steered itself to a dear friend's home, who was not someone I "hung out" with regularly. She was not someone who would vocally take sides and take off after my ex to show him what she thought. That would be my sister, my greatest ally. No, this person was not even on my mind. God drove my car to her house. I cried. She listened. I sought her advice. I will never believe God causes bad things to happen to us, yet He uses these things for good. The pain my friend had gone through in her first marriage, she grew through and used to help so many others. She held me, and I felt a peace with her. You must intentionally choose good people to be with and listen when God sends some to you.

I had another group of people who were amazing during this time. They were my small group bible study. The ironic thing is this was the couple's study group my ex and I had been a part of. We were all close and still are. I cannot begin to write all the things they did for me individually and collectively during this time. One beautiful example of the love they had for me that demonstrated God's love in such a special way, I would love to share with you. My oldest daughter played soccer and was going to have a game on her birthday. Her father was going to bring his new "friend" to her soccer game. This would be the first time I would have to see them together. Needless to say, I was not looking forward to this, especially on my daughter's birthday. This is my daughter's birthday; I remember thinking.

She should not be a part of this so soon; I clearly remember the hurt as I talked inside my head. However, I kept those thoughts to myself, and I mentioned them coming to the game to one of my friends in the small group and asked her to pray for us that night. Of course, she said she would. She was one of those praying friends I had mentioned earlier.

That evening when we arrived early for the game, I nervously glanced up at the bleachers, so I could quickly locate a seat after my daughter was settled. While looking up, I saw something I will remember forever. Sitting there were the couples from my Bible study group. They had arrived early and were sitting in a horseshoe shape with an empty seat surrounding where they saved for me to sit.

Talk about being surrounded by God's love! No one else had to know the significance. Whether they intentionally meant for me to see that, I did not know until later. I saw it and the anxiety melted away. Following the game, they still embraced my ex-husband, and politely met his new girlfriend. I lovingly watched my friends embody Christ at all times, while I carried with me the vision of being surrounded by their love, and God's, from that time forward.

The same person who arranged for everyone to meet at the game also took the whole day off the day my divorce became final. She traveled with me to the bank, the school board, insurance offices, and made me eat lunch. Her clear mind, loving heart, and a list of things we had to do to switch things over to my name and other legal things that must be taken care of, made this day so much more tolerable. The most memorable part of the day was in the car-rider line that afternoon as we were waiting to pick up my oldest daughter from school. I was a tired, emotional, worn-out mess. While sitting in the line, she took my hand, and we prayed. She prayed, I should say. She prayed for me. She prayed for my babies. Strength came back through that prayer. I remember clearly to this day how that prayer and that moment felt.

Blessings came through an incredible group of friends I taught with, too. They rallied around me with an impromptu sleepover the day my divorce papers were served. They loved and supported my children in ways I can never place a value on. They made sure I had invitations to everything, so I would never be alone on holidays or birthdays. There were always shoulders to cry on, phones that would be answered in early morning hours, fixups, cold shoulders to my ex in masses, and some of the best friends of my life. Make sure you have friends who will surround you, pray for you, and support you through times like all of these. I know these times will come for you. Maybe they already have, I pray you to have a support group already in place to surround you. Be intentional about your day-to-day choices and never travel the road alone.

The Truth About Fairy Tales

Now, how does all this tie into fairy tales? Webster defines a fairy tale as: "*a story involving fantastic forces and beings. It is a story in which improbable events lead to a happy ending*". Since we were little girls, many of us heard the words, "Once upon a time". We read about or were told of princesses and queens who lived in faraway lands. There were always evil forces at play to somehow ruin the lives of our fearless beauty and prevent her from being happy. And let us face it; some of the villains in these fairy tales were plain wicked! They inflicted pain, stole, cheated, and even tried to kill to get their way. Does this mirror real life? I say, yes, it does. As a first-time mother of a baby girl years ago, I was determined to encourage my daughter to choose her toys when she was old enough to choose. Although she had toys of all different types, I was not going to push gender-specific toys on her. One day I walked into the family room and found my almost-two-year-old feeding an ugly biker troll doll with an eye drop bottle. She had chosen to be a mommy, and I was excited! I ran right out and bought her dolls, bottles, and everything she needed to be a little mommy.

My mind still was not made up about fairy tales, but she made her mind up very quickly, as did my second daughter. They were dressed in princess dresses and crowns before I could say a word. They were swept up in reading "The Little Mermaid", "Beauty and The Beast", watching the movies, and soon discovering the older fairy tales before I knew what happened. It was almost a rite of passage for my little girls. Fairy Tales invaded our home for years with my daughters. When my son came along, he cared nothing for the girl themes in the stories, but he quickly picked up on the pirates, swords, knights, armor, and anything else he could glean from the tales since he had to watch the movies and listen to the books with his sisters. This continued with our oldest granddaughter, and today our little 3-year-old granddaughter believes she is Jasmine. This is not just a little girl thing. It is often a grown-up girl thing, too. The prince riding in on his white horse or luxury automobile today, arriving at just the right moment to rescue the princess, is still the theme in most romantic movies we watch and the books we read.

Face it. It is about love and the majesty of the story that we are drawn in by and what we base so much of our lives on as women. This is often what gets our hearts broken first. The prince on the white horse is just a man. The horse is not a thoroughbred. There is no palace. No matter how nice the house is, it is going to cost money, and it is going to need cleaning. There are usually no servants. Nobody follows all your orders, or at least not for long. You cook and clean for yourself and guess what else. You are not that perfect princess, either. What? Have you never read that version? No one would buy that book if it were for sale, would they? We desire to try to be as close to perfect as possible, and we hope for that kind of life.

Most people will tell you then that the truth about fairy tales is that they are not true. I have to say that I disagree. Now, I agree that the Disney versions of fairy tales or the Hans Christian Anderson versions are not true, but I believe there is another story that matches the true definition, and it is this "Truth about Fairy Tales" that we as women need to hold on to and share with younger girls. If you are on the road to healing now, you especially need to hear this.

Prayerfully read these words. The truth about fairy tales is our story; our story involving *fantastic forces and beings in which improbable events lead to a happy ending* is true. So, let us take this from the beginning.

"Once upon a time:" This was your time at the beginning of your marriage. Now, you have been muddling through the events in the middle, the middle chapters of your story. This is now while you are at this crossroads in your life. Here, you are trying to find the path to the road that will eventually lead you to peace and healing. This is where it gets good. We need to leave these middle chapters and move on to the best part of our story. Are you ready? Next. "There was a princess."

This is the beautiful part that the Bible teaches. This is where we are missing the "enchanted and fairy tale symbolism" if you will, of our lives. This is where our lives will begin our fairy tale comparisons. We become so burdened by all we are going through. Believe me, I understand this and acknowledge there are serious issues to face in our world and our individual lives. However, we, as strong women, must claim our rightful titles and begin living in this realm where God our Father wants us to live. The facts are the facts. God is our Father. Do you believe that? God is our Father, and He is the King of all creation, the King. If He is the King and you and I are His daughters, then what does that make us? Right, it makes us Princesses. If that is not enough evidence, our Lord Jesus is the Prince of Peace, God's Son. If this is true, and He is a Prince, then we are His Princesses.

I can almost hear skeptics reading this because it takes so much to believe and see ourselves in this light but let us continue. Every good tale has a villain. The villain wants to undo the royal family in some way and usually will stop at nothing until this occurs or they think it has occurred. The Bible speaks of this in Ephesians 6:12. Now, please hear me say this. Scripture is not a fairy tale or any other type of tale. It is God-breathed and is in no way a tale, and I would never lessen the holiness of God's Word by giving it the same value as a fairy tale. However, the words in this scripture clearly tell of this spiritual battle for our hearts that is ongoing. This is more powerful and exciting than anything else ever written outside of the Bible.

Ephesians 6: 12: *"For our struggle is not against flesh and blood, but against the rulers, against the authorities, against the powers of this dark world, and against the spiritual forces of evil in the heavenly realms."*

There are two princes battling for our hearts and eternity, but if you have read the book, the Bible, you know how the story ends. This is real.

Human eyes cannot see the battles that ensue daily, but we can rest assured that they are happening and that the "bad guy" in our stories may score a few points at the end of the day, but he will not win. Jesus will not allow Satan to win our hearts. The winner of this battle has been known since the beginning of time. This is not a fantasy or a tale, but it is a real story, and we are real characters who are a part of the greatest story ever told.

The first chapters of our stories were the beginning of the "fairy tale" of our marriages. The middle chapters are the dark days of the separation and divorce. The end chapters are not the final days of our story but the new beginning chapters that hopefully will be full of love and adventures that surpass our imaginations and hopes and will eventually last eternally. Finally, one day you will be ready to turn the page. Even though you may not be there yet, and that is okay, one day you will be ready to end the tumultuous and painful journey of these middle chapters and begin the end chapters of your story. Unless we handle our middle chapters wisely, these end chapters will not be all they can be. Unless we totally understand the concept of what the real meaning of "fairy tale" is for us, our end chapters will not be all they can be.

Philippians 4:4-7: *"Rejoice in the Lord always. I will say it again, rejoice. Let your gentleness be evident to all. The Lord is near. Do not be anxious about anything but in everything, by prayer and petition with thanksgiving, present your requests to God and the peace of God which passes all understanding will guard your hearts and your minds in Christ Jesus."*

The peace of God will guard your hearts and minds. Think about this for a second. What a promise. He promises us He is near, so be happy and rejoice. Do not be anxious but talk to Him about everything, and He will guard us. Made for TV fairy tales probably will not show the king or queen lowering themselves to do this, but our King can and does. The Disney version of fairy tales might not show the princess wearing jeans, grocery shopping, vacuuming, wiping noses, and changing dirty diapers. She is probably never shown mowing the lawn, sitting at night alone waiting for her phone to ring, or eating at a restaurant with a couple who are her friends while she has no one. All or some of these may be your reality at this time. If so, let us look at these same scenarios with your crown on. What if you were worldly royal? Would you feel different about those situations? We as women need to get used to seeing ourselves as royal as we go through our day-to-day lives on our good days as well as our not so good days.

Once again, while writing about our lives being compared to that of a fairy tale, I am not comparing God's Word and fairy tales. I do not mean to take anything away from the incredible worth and importance of the scriptures by comparing them to fairy tales or any other types of writing. I am just pointing out the definition of fairy tales and how it mirrors the characteristics of how the Bible describes the battles being fought that our eyes cannot see and how we are children of the King. Fairy tales are hundreds of years old and are known world-wide, yet the stories themselves have been rewritten time and time again. This has occurred because these tales are made up of stories, and they are retold and rewritten to match the needs and times of society. The Bible is not a fairy tale. Unlike fairy tales, we read as a child or see at the theater, the Bible does not change with the times. While you may read two or three different versions of "Aladdin" or "The Little Mermaid", there is only one version of the stories in the Bible, and they never change. Yes, the wording may vary depending on the translation of the Bible, for example, the wording of the King James Bible as compared to the New International Bible, but the characters and stories cannot be changed because God himself breathed the words to be revealed in the scriptures. A thousand years ago or a million years from now, women will be able to read the same stories of Rachel, Lydia, Sarah, Hannah, and other heroines in the Bible and be impacted by them in the same way.

Having said that, imagine how it would be if we began each day in prayer and Bible study with our Heavenly Father, acknowledging our relationship with Him as His daughters, our place in His heart, and His role in our lives. Then imagine if we believe it and live it. Just think, we are sharing the same Father with all those amazing sisters in the Bible. Talk about a good family tree! If our mindset changes and we understand that we are captivating, lovely, and royal, we can make it through anything with His peace. We need to understand He *was* loyal, He *is* loyal, and He *will always* be loyal. Rest in this assurance. We do not see that storyline in Hallmark movies.

When we are alone and running through our mundane tasks, wearing a tiara may pick us up and serve as a reminder. Wear one while driving or have a group of girlfriends wear them as reminders. Begin to live out these chapters and help others live out theirs, too. For encouragement, take time to read some of the stories of how our Father loved the women of the Bible. Remember how He *never* changes. We must believe and trust that is what He is hoping for and waiting for.

Sister, this world is a beautiful place. Have you ever stopped to think that our Father could have created everything in black and white, and we would have never known the difference? Yet, He took deliberate care to make countless shades of each color. He could have created one kind of cat, dog, frog, or butterfly. Still, He took those colors and designs and created more types than we can even count. Think about snowflakes, fingerprints, clouds, and stars. One of the parts of the book "Captivating", that brought everything together for me was considering all of the majesties of the world. After all of creation, was complete God and Adam were together admiring the beauty of creation yet something was missing. Something kept all of God's creation from being perfect. One thing was missing: a woman. We are the crown of creation. How often do you feel that special? I am sure after what you have been going through, not very often. It is time for that to change.

This is a magical story that we are all a part of. We are that special. You are that special, and we must begin seeing ourselves through those eyes. Your chapter right now might be the part that you want to end very quickly. I hope it will. Christian sisters must stick together in these and all times. We must see us for who we are: Sisters in Christ who will share a home in Heaven forever. We need to raise daughters and granddaughters who will always see their worth and will learn to build up other sisters.

A Facebook post recently circulated that said, "When you straighten a sister's crown, do it without telling others why it was crooked". How true is that statement, and how uplifting would a life like this be? Always stand beside and around each other, so that our sisterhood demonstrates the love of our Father and dictates what we do and how we help others. If we live this way and truly believe this, then the mundane of every day will be brighter.

The pain of separation and divorce will dull a little faster, and the love we give others who may be going through this same pain will help them rise faster and be the strong women God intends all of us to be. I cannot tell you that every day will be easy or even manageable. That is not true. You already know that some days just breathing can seem like a victory. I wore my knees out praying. I wore three pairs of shoes out running. I ran so much hot water out crying because the shower was the only place, I could be alone to cry. But things do get better if you will let God and others He puts in your path, help you grow through this time. Take a stand to be strong and be determined to make it. You must also fight for yourself. So often we are so busy caring for others, we neglect ourselves. Do not get me wrong; I think we heal by serving others.

However, if you have ever flown on a plane, the flight attendant will tell you, in case there is a loss of cabin pressure, oxygen masks will lower from the ceiling. If you have a small child in your lap, or are helping someone else, *use the oxygen first before helping someone else*. Realize it is okay to take care of yourself. If you are not okay, then you cannot take care of anyone else.

Although life may seem to be put on hold while you are going through this awful time, in reality, the world continues to spin. Others continue to need you: a physically, mentally, and spiritually healthy you. A royal you.

One of the most personal scriptures to me is Psalms 66:16, *"Come and hear, all you who fear God; let me tell you what he did for me"*. This became my life lesson. I can be stubborn, but through this scripture and prayer, many things finally became much clearer to me. As I said, I had just a few friends who had been through what I was facing, so I tried to read books by authors who had been through a divorce so I could learn from them. At the beginning of this ordeal, I remember reading testimonies by writers who would say they heard God's voice and His words clearly led them to a place of healing. Others said they felt God's presence and a calm assurance about their decisions and fears. Honestly, I can tell you, as hard as I prayed, I could not audibly hear God's voice, and it took me a long time to feel that calm assurance. I remember asking God why I could not hear Him when others did? Why could I not feel assured I was going to be okay?

I realized after a long time that I was trying to live in fast motion. I wanted to fast forward through all that I was dealing with, and I wanted things on my terms, in my time. If I could just touch your robe, I remember praying, I would be at peace, and I would feel safe. I remember times trying to find a church that was open during the weekdays just to go in and pray. The rush to heal and the rush to move things along kept me from what God was trying to tell me. This was when I came across this scripture in a daily devotion. After reading this scripture, I realized that God was speaking to me through others who had been through their own middle chapters and had moved on to the next part of their story. God *was* speaking to me. It took me reading His words in the Bible to finally see that. Take time to listen. Just take time. These days will pass, but not until you are truly ready to turn the pages and begin the new chapter in your life.

Psalms 66:16: *"Come and listen, all you who fear God, and I will tell you what he did for me."*

The Bible is full of beautiful words to remind us of our role in our "fairy tale" if you will, that we are blessed to be a part of. If we as women, especially women who have been through the ache of divorce, could claim scriptures like Ephesians 2:10 and truly believe it, our healing would be more complete. So often, too often, we judge ourselves by a mirror. We judge ourselves by others' standards, and sadly we judge our worth by the one who walked away from us. We judge ourselves by others' expectations and not by God's Word. If we will claim and really believe God's words in the Bible and take care of this precious gift of our body that God created and knit together for us, then I believe our purpose and calling will be easier to see and carry out, even after divorce. Our broken hearts will heal faster. We will love ourselves more and judge ourselves less. Let us use the mirrors into our souls and fewer mirrors on the wall or reflections that we see in others' eyes as we conclude these middle chapters and move into the part of our stories that will bring happiness and wholeness once again. Let us prayerfully believe Ephesians 2:10, *"For we are **God's handiwork**, created in Christ Jesus to do good works which God prepared in advance for us to do."*

You are loved, valuable, precious to God, and others. Notice the beauty of the day and the peace of the night and know that God made both for you. Walk straight and keep your eyes on God and the peace that waits for you. Remember that someone else cannot give you that peace that comes from God, it must be inside you. Someone else cannot do that for you or make you happy. To be able to appreciate the love of someone else someday and handle the, "For Better and For Worse", you must be whole. So, do not rush, wait, and be patient for healing, even when it seems like the road will never end. It will end, and you will love what is waiting for you there.

Fairy tale princesses may possess qualities that we have grown up wanting to emulate. Our girls today may be faced even more with this with the multiple Disney movies saturating the market. I do not think this is altogether a bad thing if we remind ourselves and them of the beautiful spiritual perspective that we must have. Combining some of these characteristics and a spiritual perspective is healthy during this time of change during a divorce. Having the intelligence of Belle, the curiosity of Ariel, and the bravery of Mulan will serve us well. Remembering the helpfulness of Cinderella, the faithfulness of Anna, the respectfulness and appreciation of God's beauty in nature that Pocahontas realized, along with the adventurous spirit of Rapunzel, will help us serve others and refresh our spirits. Being kind like Snow White, using our talents like Aurora, (and taking a good nap), standing up for yourself like Jasmine, having dreams and goals like Tiana, and having a free spirit like Merida (from time to time), will exercise the creativity and individual gifts God created each of us with.

While these are commendable and encouraging traits and we would be wise to strive to have all of these qualities, remember, God has made us in **His** image, which consists of all of these characteristics and more than we could ever fathom. 1 John 3:2 so beautifully reminds us:

"Dear friends, now we are children of God, and what we will be has not yet been made known. But we know that when Christ appears, we shall be like him, for we shall see him as he is".

Sister, please remember this. *No* person, *no* circumstances, *no* hurts, and *no* memories are stronger than our Father, who created you to be like Him.

Psalm 139, the entire Psalm, is a beautiful reminder of this. The most memorized scripture in this passage is Psalm 139: 13-14: *"For you created my inmost being; you knit me together in my mother's womb. I praise you because I am fearfully and wonderfully made; your works are wonderful I know you full well."*

Although these words are an intimately loving and inspiring reminder of our royal beginning from our Father, the entire passage Psalm 139 is a love letter, a poem, reminding us of how much our Father adores us. "...He knows when I sit and rise", "...I can't flee from his presence", "...His hand will guide me on the wings of the dawn", "....The darkness will not hide me", "...The night will shine like day, so I'm not hidden from you", "....Your thoughts of me outnumber the grains of sand", "...Lead me in the way everlasting".

Take a moment to reread those last words, "...Lead me in the way everlasting". This is our happily ever after. What an incredible gift to know that the King of all Creation, your Father, wrote your story before you began your life.

This world had, has, and will always have trouble. However, just like our favorite fairy tales end happily, for those who love God and know His precious Son, Jesus, we have a real ending that we can keep in mind as we go through our story. This is not a made for TV story, soap opera, or movie. This is our story that features the fantastic forces of our Lord and Heavenly Father, angels, and strong Christian women banding together to make what seems like an improbable event of surviving divorce lead to a happy life. This is so much more than make-believe. Oh, my goodness, what a tale He has in store for you.

Remember that He has written your story. Someone else may have grabbed the paper, scribbled on it, marked out many of your words, and tried to rewrite the ending you had hoped for. They may have torn the edges when they ripped it from your hands. Did they cause it to be wrinkled, worn, or torn in pieces? Give the page back to God now and He will put the pieces back together. Quit trying to write your chapters or steal the pen from the Author of all Creation. You will live happier while you watch what He writes, unfold in your life. While you are living your story that He has written for you, not only will you be, still standing, yes, you will live happily ever after.

2 Corinthians 4:17 "For our light and momentary troubles are achieving for us an eternal glory that far outweighs them all.

Shelia Horton

sheliaahorton@icloud.com

Shelia Horton has a passion and desire to assist women in stepping into their destiny and fulfilling their life calling. She has served in ministry for 10+ years, and she currently oversees the Women's Ministry at her local church. Shelia also values time with family. She has two sons, Terrell and Branden, two amazing daughters-in-law, Katherine and Lauren, and two grandchildren, Connor and Braylon.

Shelia is a native of Wilkesboro, North Carolina, and she is a veteran of the United States Army. God has rewritten her love story, and Shelia has met and married the love of her life, Kerry. They currently reside in the state of Kentucky.

Favorite Scripture

Philippians 4:13
I can do all this through him who gives me strength.

Dedication

This chapter is dedicated to my family. You all believed in me and encouraged me to write my testimony. Thank you for your support and unconditional love.

The Other Side of The Mountain

By: Shelia Horton

The Bottom of The Mountain

There have been times in my life when I have felt like I was facing an impossible mountain. I felt like I was at the bottom of the mountain looking up and wondering how I was going to get to the other side. Life was throwing things at me that I was not prepared for. As soon as I would start to climb the mountain, life would knock me back down to the bottom, but I refused to give up. I had a choice to let these circumstances be a stumbling block or a steppingstone. Just one step, even if it were a baby step, even if I had to crawl, I would be one step closer to the other side. There were days when I did not move at all, and there were days when I made ground. There were days that I cried, and days that I rejoiced. There were days when I wanted to quit, and days that I felt I could conquer the world. I knew that this was not going to be an overnight journey. I was going to have to take this journey one step and one day at a time.

My First Marriage

"I want a divorce!". Those words stung me to my core and completely blindsided me. In an instant, my world fell apart. I had met my husband while we were both in the military. We were both nineteen and thought we owned the world. It was a whirlwind romance. We met on a blind date in February and were married two months later. I became pregnant on our wedding night. Things quickly went downhill. We could not afford our very own place. His sister and brother in law (also stationed at the same base) graciously allowed us to move into their basement. A few months later, he announced his decision to enroll in a university full time in another state, when his term of service was up. There was no discussion, only him telling me what he was going to do. There was a base close to the university, but I could not be transferred there due to the pregnancy. Two months later, he left for school, and I stayed an additional month with my sister and brother in law. I was able to get assistance from the military to move into my own apartment. About a month later, I was at home cleaning, and the phone rang. It was my husband. He asked me if I was sitting down, and I told him to give me a minute to do so. He then said, "I cannot accept the responsibility of being a husband or a father, and I want a divorce!". I could not believe what I was hearing. I was devastated. All I remember from that moment was hanging up the phone, calling my mother crying uncontrollably, and trying to explain to her what happened. She kept telling me to try and get my emotions together for the sake of the baby's health. I was devastated and heartbroken. Even though we had only known each other for a short amount of time, I loved him and could not imagine life without him.

The next day, I went to my platoon sergeant and explained what was going on. I told him that I could not afford to keep the apartment, and I had nowhere to go. He talked with my company commander, they made an exception, and I was able to move into the barracks even though I was pregnant. Some of the guys from my unit (I was the only female in my unit) came over to the apartment, packed up my things, and moved my belongings to the barracks. It was a tough pregnancy. Not only was I dealing with my husband leaving, I was sick the entire pregnancy. I had migraines, and I stayed sick to my stomach. I cried a lot during my pregnancy because I was experiencing so many ranges of emotions. I was angry but also hurt because my husband had left me. I was scared, not knowing what the future would hold for my unborn child and me. I was lonely and homesick for my family in North Carolina.

I moved into the barracks during the fifth month of my pregnancy. I spent my days working in the office as an administrative assistant, and my evenings in my room. One day a group of people from my unit were going to lunch at a local restaurant, and they asked me if I wanted to go. I asked them if we could stop by an ATM on the way. I went to get money, and the ATM denied the transaction. The company secretary said that she would cover my lunch and that she would take me to the bank when we got back to the base. Through my embarrassment, I tried to smile and have a good time at lunch, but in the back of my mind, all I could think about was the denied transaction. I went to the bank, and my husband had taken all the money out of our account. I did not have any money. I did not know how I was going to make ends meet. Why would he do this? How could he do this? I told some of the guys in my unit what had happened. For the next few months, the guys from my unit bought my breakfast and lunch from the base cafeteria. The company secretary invited me to her house every day for dinner. I felt like I had hit rock bottom. I wanted things to go back to the way that they were supposed to be. Could it get any worse? Just when I thought that it could not, it did. I received word that six weeks after my baby was to be born, I was to report to Korea. I would be stationed there for a year, and I could not take my baby with me. I had no idea what I was going to do. I talked to my platoon sergeant, and he suggested I seek military legal counsel. The military attorney suggested that I find a relative that could take my baby for a year. I talked with my parents, and they agreed to take the baby. While I was still pregnant, I signed the rights of my unborn baby over to my parents.

The next few months were brutal. I cried constantly, and I was still sick with migraines. I went to my seven-month checkup, and the nurse came in and took my blood pressure. She took it again, I asked her if everything was okay, and she said that she would be right back. Another nurse came in and took my blood pressure. I asked her the same question, and she said that a doctor would be in momentarily to talk to me. A doctor came in, and I asked if everything was okay. He looked at me and told me that my blood pressure was 180 over 100 and that I have preeclampsia. I told him that I did not know what that was. He looked at me and said, "Basically, your body is allergic to being pregnant. If we do not induce you today, either you will die, your baby will die, or you both will die. Do you have anyone that you can call?". I called the company secretary and told her what was going on. I asked her to get in touch with my parents. I was immediately put into a helicopter and flown to a local children's hospital. I was scared, and I was alone. Less than an hour later, I checked into the hospital, and the company secretary showed up. My sister in law called me at the hospital. She asked me if I wanted her to fly my husband in for the delivery, and I told her that I did not. However, a few hours later, he showed up. It was awkward with us both being in the same room, and I did not want him there. It was at that moment that I realized just how angry I still was at him for leaving us.

There was never any closure for me. My husband spoke the day that he told me he wanted a divorce, and that was it. I never got a chance to say how I was feeling. We had barely spoken since that day on the phone, and to now be stuck in a hospital room with him for an unknown amount of time caused me even more anxiety and stress. I was so grateful to the company secretary for staying by my side the entire 20 hours of labor. I gave birth to a four-pound seven-ounce son who was seven weeks premature. Hospital rules prevented us from leaving until my son weighed at least five pounds. My husband stayed for a couple of days after the birth, with little to no conversation between us. Every time I looked at him, anger rose within me. I felt my best course of action was to remain silent, not cause a scene, and not embarrass myself at the hospital. My main concentration was my son and making sure that he was healthy. After he left, my son remained in the hospital a few more days and was able to go home after a week. After being released from the hospital, my son and I boarded a plane the next day and flew to North Carolina. I was so nervous on the flight with a newborn. My son started to cry, and I could not get him to stop crying. I then started to cry myself because I could not get him to stop crying. The stewardess came by and asked me if she could be of any assistance. I was crying so hard that I could not speak any words. She looked at me and asked if she could hold him. She held him and rocked him until he stopped crying. She would periodically check on me during the flight. Once we landed, my emotions overcame me. My mom and my grandmother picked me up at the airport. I was so happy to be with my family. I felt the weight of the world lift off my shoulders because of the love and support of my parents and grandmother. During my third week of maternity leave, Desert Storm broke out. I feared going to war. I received notice that my orders to Korea had been canceled. Not knowing what would happen when I returned to the base, I left my son with my parents.

My Relationship With God

For the next six months, I spiraled downward. I was going through a divorce, my parents had custody of my son, and I started to party like I had no responsibilities in life. I was an angry and bitter person with no sense of direction. I was still upset and hurt at my husband for leaving. My mother always reminded me to depend on God. I grew up in church, and I heard her, but I was not listening. I continued to do what I wanted to do. Turning to God was the furthest thing from my mind. I wanted to live my life, my way, and on my terms.

My Second Marriage

After my divorce, I quickly started to date again. I was still at my current duty station in the U.S. Army, and I began to date one of the sergeants in my platoon. It became serious, extremely fast, and a few months later, I was pregnant again. The circumstances were not ideal because my oldest son was six months old when I became pregnant, and he was still living with my parents. He had a daughter who was also six months old. I was living off base with a roommate, and a few months after we found out about the pregnancy, my roommate moved out of the apartment, and he moved in. The following month, I drove to North Carolina and picked up my son and brought him back with me. I was incredibly grateful to have help in raising my son. He helped me raise him even though my child was black, and he was white. He never treated him any differently. He treated him as if he were his biological son.

Life was incredibly challenging. His daughter from a previous marriage and my son were born in the same month and the same year plus we had a child on the way. He had child support obligations that he paid each month faithfully. However, I did not receive child support from my son's father. Finances were very tight. There were times when we could not afford diapers and formula. I felt humiliated and like a failure because there was not enough money to provide for my children. I would call my parents, and they would help us out financially when we could not make ends meet.

This pregnancy was just as rough as the first one. I was sick a lot and displayed the same symptoms as I did with my first pregnancy. I went to a routine doctor's appointment. The doctor explained that I had preeclampsia again, and my blood pressure was high. A helicopter immediately airlifted me to the nearest military hospital, one state away. I informed the company secretary of the situation, and she said she would be in route. The nearest military hospital was three hours away. I also called my mom and told her what was going on, and she caught a flight to come and get my youngest son and take him back with her because we did not know how long we would be in the hospital. I went through labor and delivery alone because my son came quicker than expected, and my son's father was at the airport picking up my mom. The company secretary was still in route. When my son was first born, I did not hear him crying, and they did not hand him to me. Instead, they rushed him over in the corner of the room. I kept asking if everything was okay and no one was answering me. What seemed like a lifetime was probably only seconds, but eventually, I heard him crying. The doctor informed me that due to my son's prematurity, his lungs were underdeveloped, and he needed to spend time in the neonatal intensive care unit (NICU). I was so confused and heartbroken at the same time. I was confused because although my son was premature like my first son, he weighed more, and I was heartbroken because I did not get to hold him right away. He was taken immediately to the NICU. I will never forget the first time that I saw him, hooked up to a machine with many tubes attached to him. All I could do was weep. My son spent the next thirty days in the hospital. I was released from the hospital a week later. I did not know what to do. I could not afford to spend thirty days in a hotel, so the hospital arranged for me to visit for two days and go home for four, and I could stay at the hospital. Every four days, I would drive three hours to the hospital and spend two days with my son. We finally got to bring him home after the month was over. My parents kept my oldest son another month to give us time to get settled into a new routine.

During this time, I had strayed so far away from my morals and beliefs that were instilled in me as a child. I knew I was wrong in the choices that I was making. I knew that I was not living a life that was pleasing to God. There were even times when I felt convicted over my choices, but I would brush it off and continue in my current lifestyle.

One day my mom calls and says that she needs to talk to me. She proceeded to tell me that she went before the church and had my membership revoked from the church because I was living with a man that was not my husband. I was hurt, and I was so angry. I remember saying to her that the church kicked me when I was already down instead of helping me. Even though deep down inside, I knew she was right. I wanted nothing else to do with the church. Sometimes I attended services at a local church, but at that moment, I decided that I was no longer going to go. My family had become friends with a neighbor that lived up the street from us. He would take his nephews to church with him on Sundays, and he asked me if he could take my boys with them as well. I allowed my boys to go every Sunday with our neighbor, but I wanted no part of it.

I continued to live with my youngest son's father for the next nine years. We had a lot of ups and downs. We fought quite a bit. I was not the easiest person to get along with, and I made a lot of mistakes and rash decisions that caused those arguments. We separated and moved into separate households for a few months. Still, we reconciled and decided that we would get married and make this work. We even started going to church as a family. Things began to turn in a positive direction. This time things were going to be different. This time my marriage was going to work or so I thought.

"I want a divorce!". When he first said it, I thought he was joking. All these questions started running through my mind. Am I hearing these same words for a second time? How did we get to this point? We had been together for ten years but married for less than one. How was I going to raise my boys? What about my oldest son, who is not his biological son, that he has raised since he was two? What about his daughter that had been part of my life since she was one? It was like time stood still. I looked at him and asked if he were joking and he said no. I then asked why, and his response startled me, "I thought you would change". I looked at him puzzled and asked, "What do you mean you thought I would change? We have been together for over ten years!". I never did get a clear answer from him as to what had changed or had not changed. I was hurt, and I was angry. I felt like my world had turned upside down. I felt so alone. I had no family in Kentucky except for him and the boys. The friends that I was closest to were friends that I acquired through him, so when we separated, I lost all those friends. I thought many times about packing up my things and moving back to North Carolina with the boys, but I just could not do it. I did not want them to grow up away from their dad. Their dad and I talked about it, and I told him my thoughts about moving back home where my family is for support. We made a vow that day that regardless of how things were between us that we would do our best to co-parent and raise the boys, and that included both boys. We promised that neither one of us would ever say anything negative about each other in front of the boys.

We were not initially financially stable to separate and maintain two separate households, so we chose to live under the same roof until we could so. We stayed in different rooms. It felt like we went from being husband and wife to roommates. It was very awkward, but we made the best of the situation. We would pass by each other and speak and then go about our daily routines. We had not told the boys and were not going to say anything to them until he was ready to move out.

That day came a few months later. He found an apartment. The boys and I were going to remain in the house. We sat the boys down and told them that we would no longer be living together. We told them several times during the conversation that it was not their fault, but they were both visibly upset and with good reason. It was at this point that the reality of the divorce started to settle in. Going through a second divorce, I felt like I was facing an impossible situation, and again my world was falling apart. The transition was tough. We tried our best to stay true to our words and co-parent. The boys went to visit their dad every other weekend, and the other days remained with me. Life was challenging. There were days that I could not get out of bed and function.

I had a small in-home childcare center with six children, which allowed me to be able to make a living and be home when the boys got out of school. They would be home with me during the summers, so childcare for them would be one less worry. On those days when I could not function, my best friend at the time would come and help me as much as she could. She helped by taking the boys to their sporting practices throughout the week, and she also helped me whenever I needed her.

Single Parenting

After the divorce was final, the boys and I had to move out of the house that we had been in for quite a few years. The divorce decree allowed for me to have the option to purchase the home under my name alone, but I was not financially stable to do so. I had mixed emotions about the move. I felt awful that I had to move them away from our home and our neighborhood friends, but on the contrary, I thought that maybe we just needed a fresh start. We slowly began to settle into our "new normal". The boys started to make new friends, and we liked the new neighborhood. I continued to keep children in my home, but I also had to pick up a part-time job in the evenings and on weekends to make ends meet. My best friend stepped in, keeping an eye on the boys, the days that I had to work. I was mentally and physically exhausted, but I had to keep going for my boys.

My Relationship with God

A Reintroduction to Church

Unfortunately, my "new normal" did not include God. At a time when I should be turning to God, I began to run away again. How could you feel like you were doing everything right, and then God let it fall apart? Where was He when I needed Him? Why did He let me go through another divorce? I was so angry at God, and I became a very bitter person. There were times when I started to feel hatred in my heart towards both of my ex-husbands. My oldest son's father was not a part of his life, and I could not understand why. I could accept that he no longer wanted to be with me, but I

could not accept that he did not want to have anything to do with his son. What kind of man can just walk away from his child and show no remorse for his actions? There were days that I wanted to pick up the phone and curse him out, especially on days when my son would ask about him. My youngest son's father started to date again, and it caused a huge rift in his relationship with both boys. One day they came home crying from their weekend visit, saying that their dad had a girlfriend. They told me that their dad had been telling them that he and the woman were just friends, and then they caught them holding hands in a department store. They were heartbroken, and I was livid. I remember picking up the phone, and when their dad answered, I blasted him and hung up on him without giving him a chance to respond or defend himself. I hated him that day because of the pain that my children were going through. I also realized that there were emotions that I still needed to address. Feelings that I had tucked away resurfaced. The reality that he had moved on without us slapped me in the face that day, and it hurt. Life was never going to be the same for any of us. The boys started to refuse to go to their visits with him because they were so angry at him. Their dad and I talked and decided that it would be best to give the boys time to heal from this. I thought that it was a very selfish move on his part because now he was free to do whatever he wanted with his new girlfriend without having to deal with the boys. Nevertheless, deep down inside, I knew that he wanted what was best for the boys and wanted to give them time to heal. I wanted all this pain to go away.

I started to hang out with a new group of friends that liked to party. I guess it is true what they say about how old habits die hard. As a teenager, I was a parent's worst nightmare. I was very rebellious, and I liked to party with my friends. I would party every weekend as a teenager, even against my parents' wishes. I felt like

I was "reliving" my teenage years. I first began to party with my new friends on the weekends that the boys were with their dad. Soon after, it became an every weekend occurrence. Heading down a path of familiar destruction, I justified my actions by being "supermom". Overcompensating care of the boys included never missing a sporting event, school event, and attending social events with friends. I refused to let them suffer in any way because of my current lifestyle. On the outside, I was this happy-go-lucky person, but, on the inside, I was miserable. Something needed to change.

Once we got moved and settled into our new neighborhood, my next-door neighbor and I quickly became friends. She had two boys in the same age range as mine. She invited us to go with them to church. As a result, I was very reluctant, but she was persistent. I finally gave in and agreed to go. I was so nervous about going. I was not sure that I wanted to walk back through the doors of the church. We went, and I was pleasantly surprised at how diverse the congregation was. It was also a very welcoming environment. We were greeted and told that there was a separate service upstairs for the children. I had never been to a church designed that way. I grew up in a small Baptist church, and we sat with our parents in church. I must admit that it was nice to sit in the service without any distractions. After the service, I went upstairs to pick up the boys, and they came running to me and telling me how much they enjoyed the service, and they wanted to return next week. Although I was not sure that I wanted to go back, I agreed to go because of their enthusiasm. Weekly attendance turned into months, and soon I found myself getting involved and volunteering in the church. I still had my doubts at times, but I knew that my boys and I needed to be in church. When I first started attending church, I continued partying with my friends, yet over time the desire to party became nonexistent. I had a long way to go in my relationship with God. Still, I was starting to develop a personal relationship with Him. This was due to the fact that growing up, I was in church every Sunday, but I did not fully comprehend what having an authentic relationship with God meant.

Swallowing My Pride / Government Assistance

While continuing to work two jobs, I was on the federal food program for my in-home daycare. This program helped pay for the cost of food for the children in my care. A representative from the federal food program came to inspect my record-keeping so I could remain on the program. While we were talking, she asked me if I knew about government housing. She informed me that I could apply for government housing that is based on my income. She also explained how I could enroll in college and further my education. The meeting with her was life changing.

I struggled with whether to apply for government housing. I had heard so many negative stigmas regarding public housing, such as the housing being in bad neighborhoods and poor school districts. I did not want to seem that I was looking for a handout, but having rent based on my income would be beneficial for my family. I struggled with deciding, but I finally decided to swallow my pride. I submitted my paperwork for government housing, and a few months later, we were approved. We moved into a 3-bedroom, 2-bath house with a fenced yard in a great school district. My rent was affordable, and we also qualified for food stamps and medical cards. I started to feel like I could exhale. What I had in my mind as a handout ended up being a saving grace that became a hand up.

Full-Time College Student/Full-Time Job/Full-Time Mom

The summer was coming to an end, and that would mean that I would no longer have children to care for in my in-home daycare. I started to reflect on my conversation with the representative from the federal food program about going to college. No one on my dad or mom's side of the family had been to college, so this would be a first for my family. I called the admissions department, and they told me how to apply. I was accepted and enrolled in the community college full time in August 2002. Returning to college as an adult presented many challenges in my courses. I would be attending classes while the boys were in school. I found a part-time job for just a few hours in the afternoon at a local childcare center in our neighborhood, and the boys were able to attend there after school. Both boys were athletes, so our evenings were busy. There were evenings when I would sit on the bleachers and study while they were practicing. There would be days when the three of us were sitting at the table together, working on our schoolwork.

During the winter of my first semester, we had an ice storm that shut down the city for about a week, and we had no power. I had to study using a battery-operated lamp because my assignments were still due. In my second semester, I began to struggle in my algebra class. I went to my professor for tutoring, and I still struggled. One day I was sitting at home, crying at the kitchen table, and my oldest son comes in and asks me what was wrong. I explained to him that I was struggling in algebra class and that I did not think I was going to pass the course. He looked at me and told me that he would tutor me. My first thought was, "Holy moly, I am going to be tutored by my 12 year old son?" and my second thought was, "What do I have to lose?". He looked through my book, and then he went and got his algebra book, and the books were almost identical. At that point, I began to laugh, and he assured me that I could do it. He was so patient with me during the rest of the semester. There were days when I wanted to give up, but he kept telling me, "You've got this, mom!". I went from a D to a C, and my final grade was a B.

I was offered a full-time position at the childcare center as the Assistant Director. I knew that it would be hard going from part-time to full-time work while attending college full-time. The position included a raise, and it was an administrative position. I accepted the job and loved working on the administrative side of childcare. There were many days I questioned my abilities, and I wanted to quit. It took me three years to earn my associate degree in Early Childhood Education and in May of 2005, I graduated with honors. It was a defining moment that validated every tear and late night. My best friend brought the boys to the graduation. I remember the moment my name was called. As I walked across the stage, I heard these two voices yell, "Go, mom!". As the crowd chuckled, I could not hold back the tears. I accomplished a lifelong goal, and to hear the boys yell as they did was priceless.

My Relationship with God

Total Transformation

During this season of being a full-time mom, full-time college student and working, my relationship with God began to change. It was during this season that I started to know God for myself. I began to not just know of Him, but I began to know Him. I would seek Him in every area of my life. I put my relationship with Him first above everything else. It was during this season that I began to learn about forgiveness and how God can heal a broken heart. Walking through this season would have challenges of dealing with issues of unforgiveness from my past. Tackling these problems directly would allow me to move forward.

Issues that I had tucked away and never wanted to face required my attention. As a child, I was molested on several occasions by some family friends. One day I told one of the boys that I was going to tell my dad. He told me that if I told my dad that my dad would not love me anymore. I believed him at first. Who would not believe him? I was only five years old. I decided that I was going to tell my dad, anyway. I got home and started to tell him, and I saw a shadow outside. It was the boy, and he was looking in the window. I did not tell my dad. I did not tell anyone until I was in my early twenties. I finally told my mom one day when I was home visiting my family. I told her because I was in town shopping and ran into one of them. He tried to hug me, and it made me sick to my stomach. I looked at him and told him that I remembered what he did to me as a child. He just looked at me, and I walked away. My mom was heartbroken by what had happened. As much as I fought it and did not want to do it, I had to forgive them. God started to show me that I needed to forgive them for me, not them, so that I could move on. It was liberating. I felt as if the weight of the world had lifted off my shoulders. It was also during this same season that I learned how to forgive both boys' fathers. I called my oldest son's father, and I told him to please just listen and let me speak. I told him that I had forgiven him for everything that he had done and that I was no longer going to hold a grudge against him. He was speechless, but I was free. I was free of the bitterness and anger that I had been carrying for so many years. My relationship with my youngest son's father began to change, as well. We decided years ago that we were going to co-parent and although we still managed to do that, we could do things better. Forgiving, my youngest son's father took our co-parenting to a whole different level. We would meet at school sporting events, and we were able to sit together and cheer our boys on without any awkwardness. I also forgave his girlfriend, who eventually became his wife. She was now the stepmother of my boys, and I felt that although this is not the norm, I needed to honor her role in their life. She treated them as her own, which allowed for the two of us to form a civil relationship. My broken heart began to heal, and as my heart began to heal, I became a better person. The healing also began to open my eyes to the fact that I needed to become an even better mom for my boys.

I was at a church conference called Driven by Eternity, and the guest speaker was John Bevere. The conference, based on his book, "Driven by Eternity", was life-altering for me. During one of the sessions, he was speaking about our purposes while we are on earth and he asked, "What would you do if you get to heaven and God asks you, What did you do with those children I gave you?". I sat there, speechless. I thought about that question for the next few weeks, and the more I thought about it, the more God would reveal how I needed to change to be a better mom. I cried a lot during those few weeks because all I could think about was the things that I had done wrong as a mom. I felt horrible and useless. Was it too late to change? Have I permanently scarred my boys due to my behaviors? In the past, I would yell to get my point across. The boys would do things just to get me off their back. I honestly did not know any better, but I wanted to do better. I became very intentional about how I talked to them, and I made it a point to listen and value their opinions. As I continued to change, my relationship with them both became stronger.

My outlook on men began to change. God began to show me that this was my season to raise my boys, and they would always come before any man. I dated a few men during that time, and they were not introduced to the boys until I thought it was going to be a long-term commitment. I had to be the one to set a new standard, therefore a man was never allowed to stay overnight at our house. If I wanted a different type of relationship, then I had to do things differently. I also wanted to set a standard for my boys.

Full-Time Ministry

Two years after attending my local church, I wanted to become more involved in ministry. I began to volunteer in the children's ministry for the church's local outreach program. The boys and I would go every Saturday to teach a Bible-based lesson to kids in a less affluent area of the city. The church had a building in that community, and we would do our weekly meetings there as well as hold events for the community.

During the Christmas season of 2006, the church held an event at the community center, and we were giving out Christmas gifts to all the kids in the community. At the event, a leader from our church approaches me and asks me if my name is Shelia Horton and what I do for a living. I told him that I am an Assistant Director of a local childcare facility. He said that the church is wanting to open a childcare center, and he wanted to know if I would be interested in applying for the position of Director. I was stunned, and he could tell because he told me to pray about it and get back to him. After the event was over, I immediately called my mom and told her about the conversation. She told me to pray on it and that she would be praying as well. I was nervous about the possibility of working in my church because I did not feel that I was worthy to work there.

My relationship with God was getting stronger, but I did not know if I was equipped for a job at my church. Although I was currently working as an Assistant Director in a church, it was not my church. I felt that I might be scrutinized or placed under a microscope. What if I could not meet the expectations of the job? After praying about it and having several more conversations with my mother, I decided to apply for the position and interviewed a few weeks later. Offered the job, I gave my notice as the Assistant Director, where I was currently employed, and I was looking forward to the next season in my life. Little did I know how life-altering my next season would be. This job took me beyond just working in a childcare facility. This position became a job in full-time ministry. I loved working in the childcare center. I loved working with children and seeing the different stages that they go through. I met a lot of great staff and parents.

Opportunities to show the love of God to the staff and the parents, but most importantly, to the children, led me to my calling in life. I loved helping people. It would bring me so much joy to see people's lives transformed. One of the first families that enrolled at the center were not attending a local church when they first enrolled their children. Over time, they began to participate in church services and eventually became leaders in the church. The first few years at my job were incredible. Showing the love of God to people fueled my passion. I loved going to work every day.

A few years later, some significant changes took place. One of the leaders in church had to resign their position, which created an available part-time position. Asked to fulfill this job, I looked at this as another opportunity to help people. Still, at the same time, I was scared and nervous that I would not be able to perform in both positions. I accepted the job and loved the position.

Teaching allowed me to see adult lives transformed through various Bible studies and classes. Things soon started to change. Facing challenges not prepared for, I began to experience a "negative" side of ministry. I thought that I was making a lot of new friends. People would invite me to lunch or dinner and events at their house. What I found out is that some of these people's intentions were not sincere. Some people would use me and try to get close to me for the sole purpose of getting close to other leaders in the church. When I realized this, I was devastated and very hurt. Some people felt that I should be there at their beck and call, and when I was unable to be, I saw a side of some people that blew me away. People were mean and cruel when things did not go their way. I was overwhelmed by the circumstances around me. Trying to not say no to any request, became my downfall. I could not keep up. Feeling stuck in a situation with no way out was exhausting mentally and physically. I was going through the motions, living a facade.

Looking at me from the outside, one would have thought that I had everything together, and I was living my best life, but on the inside, I was miserable.

During one of the Sunday morning sermons, the pastor talked about being caught up in a performance trap. He spoke about how we live in a performance-based culture. That sermon hit me like a ton of bricks. My life mimics the message. How did I get here? I am so caught up in this performance trap that I have lost my sense of self. It did not happen overnight. It was a slow fade. It started slowly, and over time I became more embedded in a performance trap. I got more caught up in doing works for God versus being who He called me to be. It took me a long time to learn the difference because when you are the one in this situation, you cannot tell the difference between the two. Things must change.

I began to pray and ask God to show me the changes that I need to make, and He honored my request and began to show me how to change myself amid my circumstances. I felt that I was starting to make some positive changes, but as I did, things began to get worse. People continued to pull on me from all different directions, and because it is my nature to help, I still could not say, "No". It was time to make some drastic changes. I began to ask God what I should do. If I were to stay where I was, I asked Him to give me the strength to endure the season and stay. If it was time for me to move forward and go in a different direction, I asked Him to please give me the courage to do so and to open a door that no man can shut. I did not get answers immediately. Months went by before God began to show me that I was going through a season change. He showed me that it was time to move forward and go in a different direction.

My Crazy Blended Family

Although things were challenging in other areas of my life, things were taking a different direction in my family life. My youngest son's dad and his wife were starting their own family. These changes in our current dynamic, put our family at a crossroads in which we had to make some decisions. Their dad and I could keep our families separate and do our own thing, or we could become an "eclectic" blended family that defies the odds of a "typical" blended family. When I say, "defies the odds", I mean, we would be choosing to share in not only the big moments in our children's lives but truly form relationships with one another. We can put differences aside and come together as a family unit. We chose to defy the odds, and I would not trade it for anything. Having lifelong family members who genuinely care about me has been such an incredible blessing. Our family dynamic was confusing to a lot of people, especially the people closest to us. We chose not to let those differences define us, but to allow those differences to make us stronger.

A few years later, my ex-husband and his wife started to attend a local church in their community and eventually chose to commit their lives to God. Devoting their lives to God was a life-altering moment for our entire family. Now that we were all committed to God, it allowed us to invest even more into our family. We all became better parents because God was at the center of our family.

Only God could have put his hand in what we consider our "crazy-blended family". While what we have is not customary and does not resemble what a blended family typically looks like, I take pride in our close relationship. Our blended family consists of several different races, ethnic backgrounds, and consists of different personalities and perspectives It is grounded in love, a transcendent love that extends beyond blood relation.

From Business Manager to Business Owner

God started to show me life moving in a different direction. He began to remind me of a prayer request from 15 years prior, which was that I one day wanted to own my childcare facility. I had tucked that request away in my heart, but the desire never left me. I called my mom and told her everything, and she said that she would begin to pray. I also contacted a close friend and mentor and asked her to pray, as well. I began to look at vacant buildings. I wanted to do this with integrity, so I knew that I could not look for a facility that was near the church. I did not want to create a conflict of interest between me and the church or the childcare center at the church. I spent months looking online, and then one day, a building for lease that was 45 minutes away from the church was vacant. I looked at the ad for a few days, and I kept hearing this little voice telling me to email the contact listed in the ad. I finally got up enough nerve to email her. I was sick to my stomach due to nerves, but I was glad that I did it. The next day I received an email response from her that the building was still vacant and that I could make an appointment to come and see it. The following week, I went to see it, and it was perfect. The building had previously been a childcare center. I took pictures and told her that I would be in touch soon. I was so excited as I was driving home, and that excitement quickly turned to fear. I had less than perfect credit, so I knew there was a possibility that if the owner of the building ran a credit check that I may not qualify. I had no money in savings, so where would I get the money to start a business and buy the necessary equipment and supplies? There was no way that I would qualify for a business loan with my current credit score. I pulled over at a rest area and started to cry.

What was I thinking? Why did I even get my hopes up? Why would God tell me to pursue this knowing my financial circumstances? I was devastated. I spent the next few days in a funk and had very minimal contact with anyone. The following week, the owner of the building called me and said he would like to meet with me and talk with me about the building. I was hesitant, but I went. During the meeting, he told me to come up with a business plan and when I was done with it to bring it back to him. I had no idea how to do a business plan. I began to research how to do one and found a quite simple outline. I began to work on it and then came to an abrupt halt.

Money!! I had no money and no way to get a bank loan. How was I going to show financial stability to the landlord that I have the money to start a business? I cried out to God to please make a way when I see no way. He spoke to me and said, "Ask your parents". Ask my parents? There was no way that I heard that correctly. My parents were both retired. Does God know something that I do not? I prayed again, and God said, "Ask your parents". I called my mom and asked her if she would put dad on speakerphone. I told them about the business plan and asked them if they would be willing to give me a business loan to start the childcare facility.

After a few days of discussions, they graciously agreed to give me the loan. I had the money, but I still did not know if I would be approved to lease the building. I called the owner of the building and told him that I had secured financing and was ready to turn in my business plan. I took the business plan to him, and he told me that he would be in touch. It seemed like time was standing still. A week later, the owner called me and asked me if I could come and meet with him. I remember driving to the meeting sick to my stomach with nervousness. I got there, and he met me at the door and told me to have a seat. He looked at me and said, "Shelia, I have a proposal for you, and I have never done this for anyone before". He slides a piece of paper across the desk and asks me to look at it. I could not believe my eyes. On that piece of paper was a proposal with a graduated lease payment. For the first couple of months, there would be no lease payment due, and payments would gradually increase, and there would not be a full lease payment due for the first year. The full payment would start after month thirteen. I read it, and I look up at him, and I asked, "So, I am approved?" and he nods in agreement. He tells me that he knows that I am a Christian and to pray on it and get back to him. I get in my car, and the tears are flowing. I knew without a shadow of a doubt that God had moved on my behalf. There was no credit check required. I was approved, and I was going to be a minority-owned small business owner.

I called my parents on the way home and told them all about the meeting. They were both so excited, and my mom said, "Look at God!". I continued to work at my church's childcare center through the summer. That summer seemed like the longest summer of my life. I would work full-time throughout the week. I would spend my weekends finding equipment and supplies for my new center and preparing the building for required inspections to open the center. As the summer came to an end, the reality that I would be leaving my job of ten years, really started to hit me.

There were days when I would get nervous and start to doubt my decision. I was so comfortable in my current position, and stepping out of my comfort zone, scared me. I had never done anything like this in my life before. I was going to start a new business in a town where I did not know one single person. Although I was solely relying on God for this new season, seeds of doubt entered my mind. What if I was making a mistake? What if I did not hear God, and I was acting out of my emotions? These questions played on my mind the entire summer, up until my last day at the childcare center. In the back of my mind, I knew that this was a "God thing", and I needed to step out and do what He told me to do and not look back. My last day at the childcare center was bittersweet. The staff and families showed me a tremendous outpour of love and support. One employee stayed with me until the last child left the center. She walked me out the door and to my car. I just stood there looking at the building, overtaken by so many emotions. Feeling sadness and joy, but then I had a peace that I cannot put into words. We stood under a tree and talked and reminisced. We reminisced and laughed about all the good times that we shared working together. We talked about God and how He has a divine plan for us both. She told me that God has big things in store for me in my next season. I took her words of encouragement and tucked them in my heart because I knew there would be days that I would need a reminder of those words. As I got in my car to drive away from the property, I began to cry. They were tears of sadness of a season that had ended, and then they turned to tears of joy of the season ahead. It was August when I drove away from the center for the last time, and six weeks later, in September, I opened my childcare center.

After I transitioned in August from being a full-time staff member at the church to be a leader in a volunteer position, the next few months were challenging. For the next few months, I fought to get to church every week. It was a struggle. I maintained some of my friendships at the church, but the reality that some people just wanted to be my friend to get close to other leaders at the church was prevalent. Some people treated me differently, and some people would not speak to me at all. I was hurt, and every time that I would walk in the door, all those hurts would come to the surface. I was standing in service one Sunday in November, and a friend of mine came up to me and hugged and asked me what was wrong. I looked at her and said, "I just can't do this anymore", and she looked at me and said, "Then don't". I picked up my belongings and walked out the door, and I did not go back. For the next year, I went through what felt like a "grieving" process. I felt like I was experiencing death. I missed my church family and friends. I felt depressed and lost. I was in mourning. I felt like I was a "spiritual vagabond". I would visit different churches, but it was not the same. I decided not to go anywhere for a few months. I needed time to heal. I started to place the blame on myself. If I had not gotten caught in a performance trap, then I would have stayed focused on God and not on works. Those works led me to place my value in people. People are not perfect, and people will let you down. I learned a tough but valuable lesson.

I decided to take some time off from attending in person church services. At first, I felt guilty about staying at home each Sunday. My mom was concerned that I would fall back into old habits and stop attending church altogether. I assured her that this was not going to happen that I just needed some time to myself. I would spend my Sundays at home studying the Bible and watching various pastors online. During this time, I reconnected with God on a level that I had never connected with Him before. I knew that

I was beginning to heal from past experiences. I could feel His presence in a way that is hard to define in words.

The next month I spent working on getting the childcare center ready to open. There were still days when I could not believe that I was driving to my own business. I met again with my landlord to update him on my progress, and he asked me if I had opened a business account yet. I had not even thought about it, so he gave me some suggestions of local banks in the area. I went to visit one local bank. The teller input the information in the computer system, and the system showed that a childcare center with a similar name currently has an account there. I asked her if there was a chance that with similar names, is there a possibility for mix-ups between the two accounts, and she stated yes. I walked out and looked up, and there was another bank within walking distance. I explained to the teller why I was there, and she looked at me and said, "Oh, wow! I am currently looking for childcare for my son". I gave her a business card and invited her to an Open House to see the facility. I walked out of that bank, knowing that was a divine moment. Sitting in my car, I cried and thanked God for that encounter. The bank teller came to the Open House and enrolled her child at the center. That child was my first enrollment. I opened the doors in the fall of 2015 with two children. A few weeks later, I had three children.

Although the doors were open, I still needed more equipment and supplies. I ran across an ad on social media for some childcare center equipment and supplies for sale. I contacted the lady, and we set up an appointment for that afternoon. At first, I was nervous because I was going to have to go to the lady's home. I had heard too many stories regarding negative encounters due to these ads. As I began to pray, I felt peace about going to this lady's house. What I thought was going to be a short visit to see some supplies and equipment turned into a two-hour visit. I looked at the equipment, and the items were in excellent condition. The lady told me that she was selling the equipment because she had retired from having an in-home childcare center. I told her that I was just starting my own. For the next hour and a half, this lady gave me so much wisdom and insight. She asked me how many children I had enrolled, and I told her three. She looked at me and said, "Listen to me, young lady. If you take care of those three children, their parents will be the ones that help you grow your business. Word of mouth is your best advertisement". I thanked her and told her that I would tuck those words deep in my heart. I walked away, knowing that God had led me to that lady.

A month later, after that encounter at that lady's house, I hired my first employee. By our first anniversary in the fall of 2016, I was almost at capacity. By the spring of 2017, I was at capacity with children on a waiting list. In the spring of 2017, one of the parents came to me and asked me if I thought about expanding. She told me that there was another building for lease on the same road as the current facility that used to be a childcare center that her child has attended. She called the landlord and got all the information and passed it on to me. The lease was doable, and the location was larger. I talked with the landlord, and he also gave me a graduated lease payment for the first few months. At the end of the summer in 2017, I opened a second location. The original location was for ages three through ten, and the new site was for ages six-weeks through two years. I hired a director to oversee the new location, and I remained at the original site.

In less than three years, I was the owner of two childcare facilities. It was as if God accelerated time for me. It was a lot of hard work, but that hard work has paid off. I would be lying if I did not say that there have been times when I wanted to give up and quit when times were hard. There are weeks that I worked for sixty or more hours. There are times that I have had to deal with employee shortages, financial issues, children having accidents that required medical attention, and parent complaints about the center. I also had to deal with cases of abuse towards some of the children by their parents, which has been heartbreaking, but I know that God has placed me where I am for this season. The good times have by far outweighed the bad times. The childcare center became a "safe place" to some of the children in my care. I have been able to provide quality care to families at rates that they can afford. I have been able to watch these children go through different milestones and celebrate those milestones. Still, most importantly, God has given me the opportunity to show the children, their parents, and the employees, the love and kindness of God. I had parents say that they never said grace before meals, that their child did not say, "Yes ma'am/sir" or "No ma'am/sir" until their child started attending the center. Countless opportunities to pray over the children and to pray with families and employees going through tough situations allows God's love to shine. Those opportunities, I would not trade for anything. During this season, I learned about God's perfect timing. When I first had the desire to have my childcare center, I was not ready. I started in childcare at the very bottom of the chain as a substitute. I worked my way up from the bottom, and although I did not realize it at the time, each position was preparing me for the day that I would own my center. I learned valuable lessons along the way. Some lessons taught me how to do things, and some lessons taught me how not to do things. God placed a mentor in my path who helped guide me through every season. I have crossed paths with some amazing people who have become lifelong friends, and for that, I will forever be grateful.

Experience Is A Good Teacher

Reflections from Childhood to Adulthood

When I reflect on my life, I think of one of my favorite books by Charles Dickens, "A Tale of Two Cities". Chapter 1 reads, "It was the best of times, it was the worst of times, it was the age of wisdom, it was the age of foolishness, it was the epoch of belief, it was the epoch of incredulity, it was the season of Light, it was the season of Darkness, it was the spring of hope, it was the winter of despair…". I know that everything I went through, the good, the bad, and the ugly, God has used to make me who I am today. He loved me unconditionally when I was unlovable. He protected me from dangers known and unknown. When I was molested as a child, God shielded and protected my mind. I was able to still function and have a "normal" life after that traumatic childhood incident. Others are not so fortunate. I have met many people who experienced the same childhood trauma that I did, and it caused them mental torture and anguished their entire lives. Some people turn to drugs and alcohol to numb the pain. Others sink into a deep depression and never recover. God has given me opportunities to speak with other women and men who have experienced the same type of childhood trauma. They ask me how I can tell my story without getting emotional, and I always give God credit for that. I remind them that I will never forget what happened to me, but I refuse to let it define me. I choose to use these situations to help others.

I reflect on when I was a teenager partying with my friends. I truly was my parent's worst nightmare. I was defiant and disobedient. I would be punished for my actions and would break curfew on many occasions. I thought I was invincible and that nothing could happen to me. As we heard gunshots and crawled out of a club and ran to the car, spared by stray bullets, God protected me. I was not supposed to be there. In fact, on another occasion, a young man was shot and killed at a club. When the police went to his mother's house to tell her of the incident, she told them that her son was asleep in bed, and there must have been some mistake. That could have also been me. I am so grateful for God's grace. I am so thankful that my parents never turned their backs on me, and they never stopped loving me.

I look back on my enlistment into the military. I enlisted in the military because I was mad at my parents and wanted to getaway. Accepted into one of the top universities in the state, my parents told me that I had to go to community college for two years first. They felt that I would most likely party and drop out of school, and they were not going to pay for me to do that. With my, "I will show you attitude", I enlisted into the military and left a few months later for boot camp. Little did I know that the military would be my lifesaver, saving me from a path leading to destruction. The military took me away from my friends, and I had no choice but to "grow up". This is not the case for some of my friends. Some of them are still on that same path today. Some are drug addicts; others are alcoholics, and some of them are in jail. That could just as easily have been me, but God had other plans for my life.

God put family and friends in my life who would give me tough love even when I did not want to hear it. Thinking back to the conversation with my mom regarding my revoked membership from the church, I never took a moment to think about the fact that I was wrong for living with a man that was not my husband. I knew it was wrong, but I did not care. It was much easier to play the victim and not take any responsibility for my actions. My mom did what she was obligated to do. Thoughts of how hard that must have been for her to stand up in front of the church and put our family business out in the open like that never entered my mind. I was only thinking of myself. That circumstance would have torn some families apart, but I am incredibly fortunate that my mom still prayed for me when I could not and would not pray for myself. She always loved me even when I was unlovable. Our relationship has grown so much stronger over the years. She is not only my mom she is my best friend.

God healed my heart and taught me about forgiveness. He taught me that forgiveness helps me to move on. As I began to heal and forgive both of my ex-husbands, I even came to a point where I asked them for forgiveness of anything that I may have said or done that caused them harm. I could have stayed angry and bitter at both of my ex-husbands, but then I would have missed out on my amazing "crazy blended family."

Only God could create our "crazy blended family". I could not imagine my life without my family. I am lucky enough to call my ex-husband's wife, one of my closest friends. After many conversations and some time together at various church and sporting events, I began to realize what an open-hearted and caring person she is. Thus, we started our strong friendship. From that point forward, I treated the children they had together like my own. They hold a huge place in my heart, and I always cherish spending time with them. Their daughter and I go on outings of our own, and every year I am invited to her birthday parties and dance recitals. Their son, who once-upon-a-time called me his "Stepmom", has always treated me like family and often asks me to attend his sporting events. I am also still close to my ex-husband's first daughter, who was born at the same time as my oldest son. We text often, and because her dad and I were together for much of her childhood, I have been able to watch her grow up, and I continue to be part of her life today. As a family, we enjoy getting together to have family game nights. We have attended both of my boy's weddings, *had the best time celebrating on the dance floor*, and we FaceTime regularly.

All the kids mentioned are so close that they do not refer to each other as "step-sibling" or "half-sibling". Even though they are not related by blood, they refer to each other as brother and sister, and that truly feels like the most gracious gift. All the sacrifices and difficult conversations were worth it for me to witness their close relationships form and build over the years. Do we get odd looks when we are out in public? Absolutely! There have even been occasions when we are out, and people will ask us who belongs to who. When we tell them, who belongs to who and the story behind it, people are amazed at our story. We have even had people tell us that they wish that other families could be like ours. We always end these conversations with, "Only God could have put our 'crazy blended family' together!".

Working in ministry full time had its ups and downs. That was a season in which I learned about God's grace. I not only learned of God's grace for me, but He showed me how to have grace for others. I would encounter a lot of people in the community daily. There were many times when I learned that the actions of others require grace. If someone is having a bad day and they take that out on me for whatever reason, I had a choice. I could retaliate with the same behavior shown to me, or I could show them grace. You never know what circumstances have happened to someone right before they encounter you. Maybe they just got yelled at by their boss. Maybe their child is acting out in school, and they just got off the phone with their child's teacher. God showed me how to extend grace through conversation. I would not respond to someone in the same manner, but I would ask them questions that showed that I was concerned and that I cared. Many times, I would find out that something happened before they encountered me and that they just needed to have a conversation with someone. There were countless opportunities for me to show grace and minister to people right where they were. God knew what they needed, and when they needed it. What an honor that He chose me to be able to minister to those who needed it.

I came into ministry with an expectation that everyone wanted to do what is best for the Kingdom of God. What I learned is that even though people are "in the church", people are still human. Some people still want or need to be in positions of recognition, and they will do what it takes to get them there. During my healing process, I learned that the way that people treat me is not a reflection of me but a reflection of them. These lessons have been valuable as I continue to serve God and serve in ministry.

When I was opening my childcare facility, He opened doors for me that blew my mind. He moved on to the hearts of my landlords. I moved into a building with no credit check or security deposit. He allowed me to find the right deals for equipment and supplies. The wisdom that the lady imparted into that day manifested before my very eyes. Those first three families were the ones who, by word of mouth, played significant roles in the enrollment at the center. To grow so quickly in three years and to make a profit each year is not the norm for small businesses. About 20% percent of small businesses fail in the first year, and I feel very blessed to have beat those odds, but I know I did not do this on my own. I had to put forth a lot of work and effort, and as I did that, God blessed my business.

God has even directed me to a new church family. A close friend invited me to her church, and I started attending there, and a year later, I became a member of the church. I now oversee the women's ministry in the church. God placed me in a position to be able to minister to women from all walks of life and to offer events that meet the women right where they are.

Each season has had its ups and downs, but through each season, I was reminded of my favorite Bible verse in Philippians 4:13, "I can do all things through Christ who strengthens me". This verse has carried me through each season. On days that I wanted to quit and give up, this verse prompted me to persevere. There are still days when I must remind myself of that verse. I look back and realize that I have finally made it to the other side of the mountain. Every step in my journey, every step up that mountain was worth it to get to where I am today.

Inspired Grace Media

Resources

If you are currently struggling with divorce or separation, the right resources can make a world of difference in your recovery.

It is our prayer that these resources bless you just in case you are lost and may not know what the next logical step is. These resources will help you figure out what your next step is going to be so that you can begin your journey to healing. We are here to help you, and I pray you contact us whenever you need us.

Taking those next steps toward the life you have always wanted to live is just around the corner.

Lastly, if you have never written before, or if you are uncomfortable writing, but you still feel like God is calling you to share your story, please contact us today to take the first step towards learning more about publishing your testimony.

Divorce Recovery Resources

Divorce Recovery Advocates for Women
www.draw4women.com
info@draw4women.com

Divorce Recovery Advocates for Women is a progressive nonprofit foundation that works to help women from all walks of life recover from the pain and turmoil of divorce. The organization was established in 2015. It was the result of a need that founder Charis Rooks found while going through her divorces. Charis found that there was a severe lack of resources for women experiencing different stages after divorce, and Divorce Recovery Advocates was born to provide these resources. Divorce Recovery Advocates for Women offers women a place where they can grow and recover, no matter where they are mentally, physically, or emotionally after divorce/separation.
Draw4Women Services Offered

- **Life After Divorce Coaching**- coaching sessions are designed to work with women in the hopes of helping them to pick up the pieces and get on their way to recovery. Our certified coaches will help you design a plan that is best for you.

- **Beauty for Ashes Empowerment Retreats**- these small retreats are meant to provide a safe space for women to share their own stories and encounter hope and healing.
- **Testimonial Open Houses**- this is a free community-based event that offers women the opportunity to come and hear first-hand testimonies of hope. The event includes guest speakers, promotional giveaways, book signings, and more.
- **Prayer Challenge Conferences**- this is an event that focuses on supporting, educating, and empowering divorced, separated, and remarried women of all nationalities and faiths in prayer. These events include guest speakers, book signings, and so much more.
- **Mission Trips**- these women trips help spread the Word of God while reaching out to women and help them in sharing their story.
- **D4W Emerging Author Scholarship**- this scholarship is aimed at helping women write and share their own stories. We have partnered with Inspired Grace Media Productions to provide women the chance to write and share their testimony of hope after divorce.

Publishing Resources

Inspired Grace Media Productions
www.igmproductions.com
info@igmproductions.com

Inspired Grace Media Productions is a Full-Service multimedia publishing company that offers an outlet through which women are encouraged to share their testimony of life after divorce. It is our prayer that God continues to use IGM as a platform where culturally diverse women can share their stories of struggle, success, hope, and determination after divorce.

Services Offered Through IGM

- **Full-Service Publishing**- we assist authors through every stage of the publishing process. We help authors build their platform through books, media, and magazines.
- **Author Publishing Advocate**- we also work to help provide our authors with an advocate to help though the process. Your assigned publishing advocate will help you through the entire process. Your advocate will be a source of motivation for you when you feel inadequate, pray with

you through issues, and help you when you are struggling through the writing process.

- **Book Sales and Distribution**- we also work with national distribution for print and electronic books.
- **Award-Winning Custom Design**- we also offer help with designing book covers
- **IGM Emerging Author Leadership Retreat**- Our authors are educated at our retreats from experienced business consultants on strategy, finance, customer service, hospitality, prayer, tithing, and fasting. Our goal is to increase our author's testimony in efforts to influence and maximize outreach potential for the kingdom.
- **Publishing Assistance**- For those that have never written for the public or are unsure of their skill or the publishing process, Inspired Grace Media can help you get your story on the right track. Feel free to contact IGM today for a free consultation. We pray with each person we meet, regardless of whether they want to continue with us for their publishing needs. We want you to feel safe and secure and to have an outlet for your story and healing.

Made in the USA
Monee, IL
03 August 2020